THE LEADERSHIP COACHING ALLIGATOR HANDBOOK

Win business with Blue Chips
and build long-term productive relationships
by playing to your strengths as a leadership coach

Kevin Oubridge
Sue Burnell

bluechipcoaching.co.uk

E-ISBN   978-095732-390-2
ISBN   978-178035-587-0

Edited by Jami Bernard, Barncat Publishing
(www.barncatpublishing.com).

Front cover, artwork and 'Fabulous stupendous' poem by Kevin Oubridge. Copyright © 2012

About the authors

Kevin Oubridge is a specialist in implementing and leveraging the value of performance management systems in large organisations. He has also worked extensively with individuals and teams in developing project stakeholder management capability.

Kevin has a Post Graduate Diploma in Training & Performance Management from Leicester University and is an accredited mentor with the government led National Enterprise Allowance scheme, supporting new business start-ups.

Sue Burnell set up Accelerated Success in 2003, working with talented leaders who want to make a real difference through driving change for business growth. Since then Sue has worked one-to-one with numerous senior leaders in UK-based and global commercial organisations. Most recently she has specialised in coaching leaders of fast growing regions of global ICT companies.

Sue has an MA in Coaching & Mentoring Practice from Oxford Brookes University and a BA in Psychology from the University of Keele. She is a member of the British Psychological Society, the society's Special Group in Coaching Psychology, and the Association for Coaching. Sue is an accredited coach with the Oxford Brookes International

Centre for Coaching & Leadership Development, and the Association for Coaching.

Acknowledgements

Many, many thanks to:

Jami Bernard of Barncat Publishing (www.barncat publishing.com), who helped us every step of the way with writing this book, from shaping the original idea through to editing the final draft.

Robert Middleton of Action Plan Marketing (www.actionplan.com), from whom we have learned so much about marketing over a number of years. Robert also taught us about 'alligator outcomes', which are statements of the value of services that really cut to the chase, and which inspired the alligator metaphor around which this book is written.

Clare Burgum of Clare Burgum Coaching, who has helped us road test many of the ideas in this book, and given invaluable feedback and advice.

All our clients at Accelerated Success (www.accelerated success.co.uk).

Contents

and *Continued Success*, and how to support them with process, tools, and marketing.

4   Focus on value – Models and methods to help leadership coaches be clear on the value they bring to Blue Chips, and how to market that value.

5   Turn leads into genuine prospects – How leadership coaches can connect with potential clients, help them see what leadership coaching can do for them, and move them closer to becoming paying clients.

6   Leave them wanting more – How leadership coaches can win business with Blue Chips using Strategy Sessions, a powerful marketing tool that is ideally suited to the coaching skillset.

7   Align with business objectives – The key steps in aligning coaching with business objectives, and how this adds value for clients and enables leadership coaches to win further business.

8   Accelerate success – How to use alignment to maximise the value of leadership coaching.

9   Measure results – The key steps in measuring the business value of leadership coaching, using quantitative and qualitative measures that have credibility with Blue Chip clients.

THE ALLIGATOR'S DANCE

The B2B of leadership coaching, and how coaches can turn themselves into business-to-business service providers

10 Leverage the relationship – How to market leadership coaching services effectively going forward.

11 Plan your transition – How coaches can manage the change from what they do now to a more Blue-Chip-friendly approach.

12 **Quick Guides** – Preparatory and supplementary coaching questions for the set-agenda meetings in the Accelerated Success Process.

13 **Additional Resources** – Useful links and further reading to help leadership coaches grow their business working with Blue Chips.

PART 1
The alligator's lament

'Why am I so misunderstood?' grumbled the alligator to nobody in particular.

Fabulous stupendous

'Ho hum', said the alligator

'It's a mystery to me

What stops me from being

The best I can be?

I've a squillion sharp teeth

In a mile of smile,

A thunderous tail

To propel me with style

I'm deceptively agile

Quick on my toes

A thoroughbred 'gator

To the tip of my nose

I'm witty and gritty

Charming and sleek

Caring of heart

Head hard as teak

I can sing, I can dance

Play oboe and drums

Spend days underwater

Doing difficult sums

I'm an artist, an athlete

A scholar right through

The inventor of String Theory

(Well, that one's not true)

Courageous, loveable

Really quite brill

My pluses are many

My failings near nil.
Such jaw-dropping splendour
I'm beginning to see!
Is it me in the way of
The best I can be?
I stick to the backwaters
Leave my drive on the shelf
Fabulous stupendous
... a bit scared of
myself?'

Chapter 1: Meet the alligator

Having a business with real bite

Coaching that focuses directly on helping Blue Chip leaders achieve business objectives is an alligator — it's swift, dynamic, and has real bite, enabling leaders to raise their game and foster higher levels of performance in those around them. It empowers them to drive immediate, significant and sustainable change for improved business results: higher levels of service, greater client satisfaction, and increased revenue and profit.

This alligator is practical, too. It can solve the most pressing leadership challenges, particularly for Blue Chips. It helps position their leaders for delivering the short- and long-term success that keep those big Blue Chips in business.

Big change! Big results!

Snap snap

Experienced and talented leadership coaches like you can expand your business exponentially by offering the high-value service of Blue Chip leadership coaching. Then why is it so hard to attract ideal clients? If this kind of coaching is a sharp-toothed alligator, why is your business not bringing in the sort of money you're worth? It's doubly frustrating, because you know that your potential clients are missing out on something of huge commercial value to them. Where did that mighty alligator go?

Unfortunately, leadership coaching is still mooching about in the business backwaters, patiently waiting for Blue Chips to leverage its true value. Sure, they use it to support learning programmes, follow up on 360, do career planning, even to fix under-performance, but few of them understand how to harness the strategic power of this specialised coaching to help their leaders reach the most challenging business objectives and improve the company's bottom line.

No wonder you're frustrated! Here's a wonderful business opportunity, and yet you don't feel able to take advantage of it. The alligator of leadership coaching is in danger of sliding back into the corporate depths to brood on what might have been.

By using this book as a guide, you are going to change all that.

Some quick Q&A before we go further

What's a Blue Chip?
Glad you asked. Blue chips are the highest-value betting chips in poker.

What's that got to do with leadership coaching?
In the 1920s, an employee of the New York-based financial information firm Dow Jones used the poker

term to describe high-value company stock. Blue Chip is now commonly used to describe stock-exchange quoted companies with a reputation for quality, reliability, and the ability to operate profitably in good times and bad.

Can 'Blue Chip' apply to other companies as well?

Yes. Blue Chip is now widely used to describe all companies that fit this image of quality, reliability and longevity. They might serve Blue Chip clients, have Blue Chip suppliers, or partner with Blue Chips.

That's quite a wide interpretation, isn't it?

It's the nature of how language evolves. This broader use of the term Blue Chip includes commercial organisations that don't quite fit the more formal definition. It even includes some non-commercial organisations such as charities, non-profits, and those in the public sector.

Really?

A company is Blue Chip if it looks, feels and behaves Blue Chip-like. Does that work for you?

Yes, thanks!

No problem.

Conventional wisdom doesn't work

If leadership coaching for Blue Chips is an alligator, how come you've been struggling along with limited success?

Perhaps you lack confidence or know-how, or you're not sure how to sell your services when it comes to Blue Chips.

And it's not like you haven't tried. You write blogs and newsletters. Attend multiple networking events and present at conferences. You chase leads, stress over chasing leads, and then try to come up with something to say on the rare occasions when you manage to get in front of one. You'd need a warehouse to store all the business cards you've been collecting and hoarding. You find yourself desperately going after business you don't even want, and when you get it, you sell your services too cheaply.

You're exhausted.

Frankly, we're not surprised these techniques haven't worked for you. You're a coach, not a salesperson! It's not where your strengths lie. It's not what you trained for, or what you enjoy. Constantly chasing after cold leads is a technique that works for some, but it's not working for you.

Why? *Because the usual solutions are no help*. They involve reinventing yourself as some sort of marketing highflier who squeezes in a bit of leadership coaching on the side. This is no way to go about selling the high-value service of leadership coaching to a Blue Chip market!

There's a reason the conventional wisdom doesn't work in your business. You struggle in marketing conversations *because you're talking to the wrong people*. You're talking to the wrong people because *you're not targeting the right people*. You're open to marketing suggestions, *but they are meant for someone with a sales background, and in a different industry.*

These approaches are just not for you. Besides, all you really want is to get on with what you do best – coaching leaders in Blue Chips to make a real difference.

Play to your strengths

We know that feeling here at Accelerated Success. In the early days of our business, we also struggled with our marketing.

Did we say 'struggled'? What we meant was we basically didn't know what we were doing. We tried things more out of hope than strategy. We tried networking events, presentations, conference seminars, exhibition stands, cold calling, free coaching sessions, in-company workshops. You name it, we tried it.

Initially, our approach was probably like yours: targeting a large audience for the purpose of funneling down to a smaller number of prospects, some of whom we might be able to convert to paying clients. Feeding that wide-mouthed marketing funnel involved a great deal of legwork just to get in front of relatively cold prospects. After that were more conversations, follow-up calls, email exchanges and meetings to identify who might actually buy. In the end, *we still had to win the business*! It was hard work, and we didn't always win the sort of business we were looking for.

On one occasion we paid for a stand at a Human Resources conference. Have you ever participated in one of those? Some of the materials and furniture you need for your stand doesn't fit in your car. We were so desperate to keep costs down we ended up struggling with large, unwieldy items on rush-hour trains. It was stressful and exhausting, and we missed the opening lunch. At the end of the day — in more ways than one — we managed to find just one measly prospect, who never signed up with us anyway.

These marketing failures, or 'learning experiences', were fairly typical for us. Looking back at our early marketing strategy, it seemed we were determined to seek out one crushing defeat after another.

As a small company we didn't employ specialists with the expertise, time and resources to generate and pursue leads and manage a pipeline of prospects, which meant we had to do it all ourselves. We were too tired to then deliver the leadership coaching we sold!

Things are quite different today at Accelerated Success. We no longer target as wide an audience as possible and funnel down to a smaller number of prospects. No more cold calling or emailing. No networking events. No endless to and fro, setting up meetings.

Today, we work exclusively with Blue Chips. A few of our recent clients:

○ **A vice president** for a global ICT company who wanted to work more strategically to grow his geographical region of the business. His coaching programme kept him focused on his top priorities for business growth, and he achieved unprecedented success, exceeding his target by more than 20 percent.

○ **A sales director** in the same company who wanted to improve how his team worked together and with other teams to speed up the sales cycle. His coaching programme helped him increase annual revenue by £7.5 million.

○ **An account director** who wanted to adopt a more strategic leadership approach to empower his team to deliver better results. Now his clients are happier and his team *'gets the deal in this quarter as planned, rather than letting it slip to the next'*, leading to a significant increase in revenue and margin.

○ **A consultant** who was leading on a critical piece of work with a telecommunications company, where the client was so unhappy it seemed ready to end the contract. Using our coaching programme, he turned the situation around. He achieved a quick win worth £400K, and positioned the account for further long-term success.

Take control of your marketing

What created the turnaround in our business?

The penny dropped just when we were wondering whether we'd have to sell the dog. We were at a birthday barbecue for the daughter of a friend of ours, Mike, a very successful salesperson in IT systems. While the kids were going bananas on the bouncy castle, Mike asked how our business was going. We spilled out our woes, and asked if he had any tips on how to sell leadership coaching.

'You don't', he said, flipping a burger on the grill.

We looked at him, aghast. 'What? You mean we should just let our business fall to pieces?'

'Not at all', said Mike. 'I mean you don't sell leadership coaching. *Your service is a solution to a problem*. Find out what problem you solve, and sell *that*.'

Now we looked at each other, our mouths agape. Mike's advice made total sense. Thus began our journey to understand what leadership coaching really is, what problems it can help Blue Chip leaders solve, and what the value of solving those problems is to the individuals we coach and to those around them — including the company as a whole. Many of our clients were in big-systems IT sales, winning contracts worth millions, so we asked them how they did it. We read the marketing and selling books they read. We tried out some of the approaches they used to connect with potential and existing clients. What we were learning was relationship selling. It's been around for years, but we were only beginning to understand how suitable it was for marketing leadership coaching.

This period of research, reflection and learning also led us to a hugely important insight into how we should be marketing our services. It was spectacularly simple:

A single coach only has the capacity to deliver 10 to 15 substantial leadership-coaching programmes per year.

This amount of business can be generated by working with a very small number of Blue Chip client companies, where the focus is on delivering top quality coaching and building long-term, productive business-to-business relationships.

To win 10 to 15 coaching engagements annually, it simply didn't make sense to go the high-volume route of targeting large numbers of new leads via networking.

This revelation led us to totally transform our business. It made much more sense to work with just a few Blue Chip clients at any time, winning further business with them and picking up referrals. You only need an optimal portfolio of three.

Your new coaching portfolio

o   One **mature client company** with whom you've worked for a few years, and from whom you can pick up most of your business

o   One **maturing client company** with whom you are building a relationship and from whom you can pick up a smaller amount of business o   A **new client company** with whom you are just starting out

Here's how it works in this new paradigm:

o   The coach builds the relationship

o   The coach generates the business

o   The coach works at all times to the coach's strengths, rather than attempting to turn into a salesperson overnight

To build your practice in a way that plays to your strengths as a businessperson and as a coach:

o   Leverage existing contacts and relationships

o   Focus on high-value marketing activity with a small number of ideal potential clients, the kind where you have a good chance of converting them to paying clients

o   No wasting vast amounts of time and energy on low-value activity where you rack up tons of new contacts, none of whom are right for you

What you need is the know-how to:

o   Grab the attention of business leaders

o   Win leadership coaching business

o   Grow long-term and profitable relationships with client companies

o   Generate further business with client companies, year after year

o   Generate new business via referrals to leaders in other companies

o   Devote most of your time to coaching leaders who, like you, want to make a real difference

o Achieve great, measurable results for you and your clients
o Enjoy (yes, enjoy!) marketing and selling as it becomes part of what you do as a coach, rather than a steel-toothed trap you dread and avoid

We now generate virtually all of our business through picking up additional work with existing clients, or via referral from them to leaders in other parts of their business or in other companies.

We don't just wait for this to happen. We make sure our clients understand the value we bring and where else they might use our services. Then we proactively seek out further business. This supplies a steady stream of prospects, all of them switched on to our service via testimonial from an existing client — such as their boss, a colleague, or a business contact.

Astonishingly, despite a smaller pool of current and potential clients, we have become masters at winning new business! Even more astonishingly, we now *enjoy* marketing and selling. We have built on our success by mapping and refining the process we follow. This helped us see that much of what we were doing to deliver value to our clients through our leadership coaching programmes — aligning with business objectives, reviewing progress, measuring success, reporting on results — was also very useful for marketing purposes. We found the overlap so great between delivery and marketing that we have combined the two into a single marketing and delivery process for leadership coaching.

That's what this book is all about.

Here you will find the marketing and delivery process for leadership coaching that we developed and use at Accelerated Success. Rather imaginatively, we call it our Accelerated Success Process. It helps accelerate success for our clients and for us, and if you follow the instructions, advice, and time-tested processes in this book, it will do the same for you.

By following this integrated process for each new coaching programme you offer, you can maximise the value of your coaching to the leaders you coach ('coaching participants'), their line managers, and the client company. *Crucially, by following this process you can also greatly increase your chances of selling further programmes to the same company and to others through referrals.*

Each step of this process has a clear purpose and leads naturally to the next step, and is supported by such currency as scripts, questionnaires, and information sheets, key elements of which you will find in Part 3 of this book, 'The Alligator's Dance'. By learning to use our Accelerated Success Process, you too will be able to target and win business with the right people and at the right companies, which will enable you to build long-term, mutually beneficial relationships that yield a steady stream of further business and referrals for more business.

Here at Accelerated Success, the bottom line is that we earn much better money doing what we enjoy, and making a very real and positive difference for our clients. We have more than doubled our rates, and don't have to work anywhere near as hard to win new business. We feel in full control over how we market our services. We target the business we want and know how to go about winning it. When things don't go according to plan — and they don't always — we know how to get back on track. We take any minor setbacks in our stride, because we are confident of success with the next opportunity.

No need to repeatedly drag ourselves up from the depths of despair. No more constantly worrying about money.

The bottom line for *you* is that you can easily learn our approach to marketing and delivery of leadership coaching. This will enable you to build a thriving leadership coaching business. If you want to generate work for associates as well, you can grow your business even more. Or you might want to go the other way, delivering just a handful of engagements each year and still earning a good income doing something you enjoy.

Soon you will see what we mean when we say we get a real buzz from our marketing. Meeting people, building relationships and winning business is *FUN!*

Chapter 2: Tales of monsters

Perilous times

Far from being a lamentable situation, the Blue Chip market outlook represents the mother of all business opportunities for the leadership coaching profession.

The global economy is vast and growing. Experts predict that by 2050 the combined economies of what have been the world's richest countries — the U.S., Japan, Germany, France, United Kingdom, Italy and Canada (still sometimes referred to as the G7) — will be overtaken by the four combined economies of Brazil, Russia, India and China (the BRIC countries). Another fifteen or so countries in Asia, Africa, the Middle East, South America and Australasia have the potential to expand their economies substantially in the same period. Not forgetting, of course, the G7 economies themselves, which haven't been eclipsed just yet, and a number of European Union (EU) countries, which either currently have substantial economies or potential for growth.

The Blue Chip contribution to these growing economies will be essential. In 2010 the total value of stock-market listed companies (market capitalisation) globally was 54 trillion U.S. dollars (*McKinsey Global Institute, Mapping global capital markets 2011*). If this figure is difficult to visualise, it might help to know that global market capitalisation in 1990 was only 11 trillion dollars. (By the way, 'a trillion' is a thousand times a billion OR a million times a million OR one followed by twelve zeros OR lots and lots and lots!) Despite a lingering global recession at the time of this writing, the long-term trend for this global market capitalisation figure is most definitely upwards. The value of Blue Chips will grow significantly over the next five, 10 and 20 years.

There are some real monsters out there. And not just a few. Lots of them. Whether you're talking U.S. dollars, GB pounds or euros, there are literally millions of companies worldwide that make millions and billions and much more. With this sort of money at stake, these are truly exciting and perilous times for Blue Chips. The rewards for success will be great and the consequences of failure unthinkable. Their challenge over the short and long term is to learn to thrive in hugely diverse and rapidly growing markets, where competition is brutal.

In this environment, a wrong step or moment of inattention could prove fatal. Company growth strategies will need to quickly translate to agile execution on the ground. Just look at Google — launched in 1998, achieved annual revenues of $16.5 billion ten years later, and just short of $38 billion in 2012. Other companies, including multi-billion-dollar powerhouses, get squeezed out or swallowed up in the rush. Between these extremes, many other companies both large and small will have their ups and downs, and few will find comfort in standing still.

There are monsters and then there are MONSTERS!

This is where leadership coaching comes in.

A critical differentiator between success and failure for Blue Chips will be the quality of leadership. Even the toughest leader may occasionally quail at the thought. Some will seriously consider a career change — llama farming in Wales, maybe. *All companies will need good leaders just to survive, and they'll need extraordinary leaders in order to thrive.* It's a chilling thought for many Blue Chips, coming at a time when they are already questioning the effectiveness of their leadership development.

According to a global 2011 survey by Development Dimension International (DDI)[1], approximately two thirds of leaders and the same proportion of HR professionals rate the effectiveness of leadership development in their company as only moderate, low, or very low. As for the existing quality of leadership, 38 percent of leaders and only 26 percent of HR professionals rate it very good or excellent. Worse, a meagre 18 percent of HR professionals believe they have the quantity and quality of leaders they'll need over the next few years.[1]

The DDI findings are alarming. Blue Chips have invested heavily in leadership development over the last 20 years. Yet, by their own assessment, large numbers of their leaders are not good enough! They have spent too much money on leadership development initiatives that have taken too long to have an effect, or that haven't actually made a real difference. Blue Chips cannot afford more of the same over the next two years, let alone twenty. They are desperately looking for ways to develop their leaders at all levels to meet the demands of the new business environment. Whatever they do must have a significant and sustainable positive impact, or they risk getting left behind.

---

[1] DDI's Global Leadership Forecast 2011 is the biggest study of its kind. It involved nearly 1,900 HR professionals and 12,500 leaders from 2,600 organisations in 74 countries.

On top of that, companies aren't in the mood to spend the sort of money on leadership development they once did, not without a guarantee of results. It is a genuinely challenging situation for all companies, in all sectors, of all sizes.

Catastrophic failure!
Bob's only crumb of comfort was
that he had absolutely no idea what
he should have done differently.

A powerful solution is right in front of them. Leadership coaching that is properly aligned to achieving business objectives delivers huge value to Blue Chips — not just for coaching participants, but for those around them, including line managers and the client company as a whole. It can foster transformational change leading to significantly improved business results. It achieves this by helping leaders put learning into practice, providing the missing link that undermines other leadership development initiatives. It helps leaders apply what they know, make the most of their experience, and get results despite all obstacles. It empowers individual leaders to make a difference, raising the bar for others to follow.

While it would be misleading to suggest that this type of coaching is the universal solution to all leadership development issues, it is a very powerful tool for overcoming the apparent inertia in developing the right Blue Chip leaders for the future.

The opportunity for leadership coaching

Now is the time for leadership coaching to show its true value. To burst out into the business mainstream and help shape the leaders that Blue Chips desperately need — leaders who thrive on the pressure and turmoil of rapidly growing global markets. Who make a real and lasting difference to their companies, their teams and their customers.

When Blue Chips get the message that this is what leadership coaching can do for them, talented and experienced coaches like you will be in very high demand. You can make it happen now! You can help Blue Chips see what they're missing and expand your leadership coaching business at the same time.

To do this you'll need to learn how to maximise the value of your coaching to your clients, then make sure they understand that value. Once they see they can get great results through your coaching, they will look around at where else in their business they might use your services. You will build long-term and highly productive client relationships, and it all starts and finishes with the value you deliver. Think back to the clients we mentioned in the previous chapter: a vice president who exceeded target by 20 percent, a sales director who increased annual revenue by £7.5 million, a consultant who achieved a quick win of £400,000. Leadership coaching was a catalyst for action and momentum in each of those situations.

And it's not just about improving the performance of individuals. Good leadership coaching enables wider change and growth. When key players raise their game, so do those around them. The changes they make stick and lead to further change. *Big* change! *Big* results! With agility! The sales director in our example achieved his spectacular success through improving how his team worked with the technical consultancy team. This led to a reduced sales cycle, quicker and bigger wins, and much more satisfied customers — and to a £7.5 million increase in annual revenue.

In addition, the technical consultancy team noticed how the changes led by the sales director improved their results too. They therefore made changes to ensure all other parts of the U.K. business could work with them in the same way, which further improved their business results.

Coaching enabled one sales director to influence business results for his team, but also for other parts of the company.

What it takes to succeed with Blue Chips

If you're worried that you don't have what it takes, here's the really good news: As an experienced leadership coach, you most definitely DO have what it takes to succeed with Blue Chips. All you need is a bit of help to make the most of what you've already got.

You ALREADY have access to a very valuable Blue Chip network through which you can connect with prospective clients for your leadership coaching services — your very own network of existing clients, past clients, other leaders you know, and learning and HR professionals. You can leverage this very valuable network of existing contacts to win business and build long-term and highly productive relationships, and to free yourself from the high-volume, low-yield approaches that take up so much of your time.

You ALREADY have the right skills and capabilities to engage with prospects and convert them to paying clients.

You're good at building rapport, listening, asking the right questions, giving others the space in which to answer, and knowing when to hold back or push harder. These are essential skills for a coach. They are also exactly the skills you need when marketing leadership coaching to Blue Chips.

We'd like this book to excite you about your potential for working with Blue Chips. It will provide you with very practical knowledge, process and currency on achieving the success you want and deserve. You will still coach in the same way you have before, but you will also be able to combine that with a real understanding of how to engage with Blue Chips to maximise the value of the relationship for them and for you.

We use exactly the same knowledge, process and currency you'll find in this book for when we market and deliver leadership coaching programmes at Accelerated Success. You have a choice: You can follow our approach closely, or you can adapt it to your specific needs. You can even 'cherry-pick' what you like and ignore the rest.

We wish you every success with your leadership coaching business. Remember to play to your strengths as a coach, rather than trying to be something you are not. Look to your existing contacts, rather than rapaciously seeking new ones at random. Service a small number of Blue Chip clients and build long-term, productive relationships.

The Leadership Coaching Alligator Handbook will help you earn the sort of money your talent and experience is worth — and enjoy it!

PART 2
The alligator's smile

Slowly, slowly, slowly, the alligator broke into a long and knowing smile.
'Aha. Now I see how I can be the best I can be'.

If you're considering climbing the Matterhorn, you probably realise you need expert advice and training. Nobody tries to climb even a small mountain without first learning a bit about what they're taking on.

You'll want to know how to maximise your chances of getting to the top and back again in one piece. What kind of clothing is best? Maybe at 13,000 feet isn't the time to show off those new sandals.

What equipment will you need? What to do in an emergency? If you don't get your preparation right, far from achieving the summit, you risk losing parts of your anatomy to frostbite.

It's the same with Blue Chips. If you want to sell to them, you'll get better results if you prepare properly. It's not life and death, as with mountaineering, but without the essential know-how of what kind of marketing works with Blue Chips and what kind doesn't, you seriously limit your chances of success. If you wing it, you'll end up being stretchered off Mount Blue Chip, which is not the way we recommend you go about building a thriving business.

In this section, The Alligator's Smile, we provide you with essential know-how for marketing and selling to Blue Chips.

Chapter 3: The power of process

The sad tale of the bread maker

Leaders of Blue Chips are out there. Vast numbers of them.

They need your help.

You're ready and willing, but whatever you do, don't try to make it up as you go along. You'll get confused, they'll get confused, and soon you will look like you don't know what you're doing. Your clients and potential clients don't run their businesses by muddling through, and neither should you, or you'll lose credibility with them.

When you work with Blue Chips, you need to eliminate the roller coaster of emotions, frustrations, mistakes and doubts. You need to know what to do in all situations.

In other words, you need a process.

A process is something that describes what to do at each step in your marketing and delivery, along with supporting currency such as a website, articles, information sheets, presentations, diagrams, email pro formas, scripts for different conversations, and questionnaires. (Don't worry — we'll help you make sense of all this!)

A sound process for marketing and delivery of your service is invaluable. Like all good processes, it eventually becomes second nature, and you won't even notice you're using it. Do you think about how to brush your teeth in the morning? How to make breakfast? Soon you'll feel like you were born knowing how to market and service Blue Chips.

Whether you're trying to connect with potential clients, get their attention, give them further information, close a sale, deliver your service, or review with them what you've accomplished together, having a process enables you to plan for every eventuality. You'll always know where you are. A process gives you position, direction and purpose — without which you are, well … LOST!

And if you ever DO feel temporarily lost, your process is there to help you quickly find your way back to familiar territory, where you can gather your thoughts and set off again on firm footing, confident in where you're going and what you're trying to achieve.

It's easy to dismiss process as something fussy that gets in the way of actually *doing* things. No doubt many processes are awful, which is why so many people are distrustful of them. Nobody notices process when it works well, but you definitely notice it when you're on the wrong end of a bad one — like the customer (dis)service call centre processes that seem designed to do anything but provide service to customers. Online processes that require you to input all sorts of information for which you have to turn the house upside down to find, at which point you click the submit button and the system logs you out.

Here's a process we recently had the misfortune to observe first-hand: We finally got our bread maker after tracking it down because it was delivered to the wrong address — only to find it had a dent in it. After multiple phone calls, mostly spent on hold listening to snippets of *The Four Seasons*, we managed to order a replacement, but it couldn't be dispatched until the dented item was returned. After several weeks of the delivery company trying to collect the damaged bread maker from the same wrong address they originally delivered it to, we gave up hope of ever having bread with our jam, so we cancelled the order and bought a bread maker from a 'proper' bricks and mortar shop. We brought it home just in time for the cancelled bread maker to arrive like an uninvited guest on our doorstep.

On the other hand, life can be blissfully easy with a *good* process. Without realizing it, we are all totally dependent on these processes. They run silently in the background as we go about our day. It has even been known to happen that a call to a customer service centre is greeted with a polite, cheery voice, and for a problem to be quickly resolved. Most online processes work without a hitch, whether for managing your finances, downloading an eBook, or sorting out flights and hotels for a weekend away. Most bread makers, we hear, are delivered quickly and intact, and can actually make bread.

This doesn't even take into account personal processes – our daily routines. When they work, things get done, or they get done faster and better. Our routines help relieve anxiety, prevent accidents, and generally make life easier.

We use personal processes when buying a newspaper, making a cup of coffee, or crossing a road.

Before they got the 'Hey diddle diddle' process properly worked out.

We rely on processes for even the most trivial things. Yet, when it comes to something that is important, complex and difficult — like marketing and delivering leadership coaching to Blue Chips — a lot of us imagine we can cobble together a few vague steps and that it will do the job.

It won't.

A good marketing and delivery process for your leadership coaching service is essential. It gives you control and confidence, and connects you with the right supporting currency when you need it.

Figuring out what's missing

Back when we were looking at how to improve our approach to marketing at Accelerated Success, we kept coming upon basic questions that we weren't sure how to answer:

When should we arrange this sort of meeting? What comes before that? What comes after? What's the purpose of the meeting? What outcome do I want? How will I set it up? What information should I send in advance? What do I have to say and do to achieve the outcome I want? How will I handle possible responses? What information should I take along? What next step should I propose? How will I close the meeting? What follow-up communications do I need? What do I need to do to move us to the next step?

It seemed we only knew the answers to these and other questions on alternate Tuesdays.

No wonder our marketing wasn't working! No wonder we obsessed each month about paying our bills! Without a step-by-step approach, we didn't know how to complete one step or move gracefully to the next. We made up process on the hoof — which was a lot of work each time around, and didn't bring in enough business. The haphazardness of our approach might not have been visible to clients, but it was visible to us, and it made our lives needlessly complicated. It's not a good feeling to walk out of a client meeting thinking you could have handled it better but aren't sure how. You're always trying to work out what's missing.

What was missing was process and supporting currency!

We needed something that would guide and support us every step of the way. So we developed process and currency to give us the answers we needed, when we needed them, so that we could market and deliver our leadership coaching effectively. Having this process enables us to win clients, deliver great value, win further business from them, and pick up referrals. We always know where we are with each client or prospect and what we need to do next to get the best results for them and for us.

By following this process we have freed ourselves from the compulsion to try anything and everything to sell leadership coaching, hoping that something would stick. We now focus on high-value activity, and don't waste time on things that simply don't work. We have the tools to do the job, and don't need to develop them anew each time. We draw on our existing network of clients and past clients to win virtually all our business.

The bottom line is that we are successful at doing business with Blue Chips. It's a great feeling!

As an experienced leadership coach you can do the same. You almost certainly already have a valuable list of contacts among leaders and human-resources specialists, and that's where you can start. You don't need to add to this list. You just need to reconnect with your contacts in a new way: Give them an experience of what your service can do for them, and then convert them to paying clients. You can then build a long-term relationship with the client company, where you win further business and pick up referrals.

The rest of this chapter gives you an overview of the process we use at Accelerated Success to do just that!

A marketing and delivery process that works

There are three phases to our marketing and delivery process:

Alignment — where we reconnect with or make first contact with a leader (a potential client), give them an experience of the value of our service, make the sale, and agree coaching outcomes aligned to business objectives.

Acceleration — where we coach the leader (the coaching participant) to achieve agreed-upon outcomes and facilitate effective communications around performance between participants and their line managers.

Continued Success — where we measure the achievements of coaching participants and help them plan actions and learning beyond the programme close. This is also where we focus on leveraging the business-to-business (B2B) relationship, enabling us to win further business.

ACCELERATED SUCCESS PROCESS

Alignment

STRATEGY SESSION
Vision & challenges

REPORT-BACK MEETING

3-WAY START UP
Links to business objectives

OUTCOME SETTING
Agreeing targets for the participant's Accelerated Success programme

Acceleration

ACCELERATED SUCCESS SESSIONS
Regular meetings and/or calls for discussion, learning & planning

Execution

Review & reflection

3-WAY PROGRESS REVIEW
Session to review progress against outcomes

Realignment

MEASURING SUCCESS
Achievement against outcomes

Continued Success

SUSTAINING GROWTH
Planning for the next 3-4 months

3-WAY FINAL REVIEW
Achievement against business objectives

REPORT-BACK MEETING

BUSINESS VALUE
4-6 months after programme close - sustained impact

REPORT-BACK MEETING

Alignment phase

Alignment

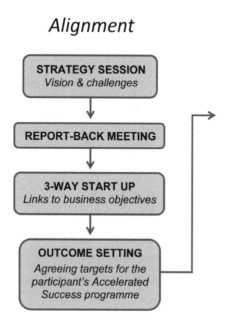

The *Alignment* phase begins with a Strategy Session. As you will find out in Chapter 6, *Leave them wanting more*, the Strategy Session is our key marketing tool at Accelerated Success. We offer these sessions free to genuine prospects to give them an experience of the value of our service. Strategy Sessions are an opportunity for leaders to step back from their role and look at their vision for their

> **STRATEGY SESSION**
> *Participant's vision, the challenges they face & how they move forward.*

part of the business, the challenges they face, and how they move forward. If the prospect goes ahead with a full coaching programme, the Strategy Session provides the first step in aligning the programme with business objectives.

Chapter 6, Leave them wanting more, explains the use of Strategy Sessions in more detail.

Following a Strategy Session, we have a Report-Back meeting. We take the participant through a summary of the output from their Strategy Session and engage them in the sales conversation.

REPORT-BACK MEETING
Summary of output from Strategy Session & start of the sales conversation.

Chapter 10, Leverage the relationship, explains Report-Back meetings in more detail.

If the participating leader goes ahead with a full coaching programme, we continue the *Alignment* phase of our process with a 3-Way Start Up meeting involving the coaching participant, their line manager, and you the coach.

The 3-Way Start Up is of real value to participant and line manager. It supports alignment and establishes a model for effective communication around

3-WAY START UP
The bigger picture! Participant & line manager discuss links to business objectives.

performance. Participant and line manager look at the bigger picture, linking Strategy Session output to business objectives. From a marketing perspective, these meetings also get you in front of another leader in the client company

— an additional potential client who gets experience of the value you bring.

Chapter 7, Align with business objectives, explains the 3-Way Start Up meeting in more detail.

After the 3-Way Start Up meeting, we have an Outcome Setting meeting with coaching participants. Previous discussion in their Strategy Session and 3-Way Start Up help them identify measurable outcomes they want from their coaching that are closely aligned to achieving their business objectives.

OUTCOME SETTING
Participant identifies measurable outcomes for their coaching programme.

Chapter 7, Align with business objectives, explains the Outcome Setting meeting in more detail.

Acceleration phase

Acceleration

ACCELERATED SUCCESS SESSIONS

Regular meetings and/or calls for discussion, learning & planning

Execution

Review & reflection

3-WAY PROGRESS REVIEW

Session to review progress against outcomes

Realignment

MEASURING SUCCESS

Achievement against outcomes

After the *Alignment* phase we enter the *Acceleration* phase, which is where the coaching participant works toward achieving the agreed-upon outcomes. Our approach is to have monthly coaching meetings, with shorter coaching calls two weeks after each meeting.

> **ACCELERATED SUCCESS SESSIONS**
> *Coaching the participant to achieve agreed outcomes.*

A key tool we use in the *Acceleration* phase is the Coaching Record, a document that is updated by the coach after each meeting or call.

Chapter 8, Accelerate success, explains more about the Coaching Record and makes the case for the coach taking responsibility for completing it.

The *Acceleration* phase also includes the 3-Way Progress Review, a meeting that continues effective communication between coaching participants and their line manager, and helps maintain alignment with business objectives. It maximises the value of the coaching to the participant, the line manager and the client company.

3-Way Progress Review is also useful for marketing purposes, ensuring that participant and line manager fully understand the difference our coaching is making. This in turn means that they are better able to see where else in their business they might use our services, and

> **3-WAY PROGRESS REVIEW**
> *Participant & line manager discuss progress against outcomes & links to business objectives.*

primes them to become powerful advocates in promoting our services to others.

Chapter 8, Accelerate success, explains the 3-Way Progress Review meeting in more detail.

The *Acceleration* phase closes with the Measuring Success meeting, which helps coaching participants identify how they have done against the outcomes they agreed for their programme. Participants reflect on where they were at the beginning of their programme, the ground they have covered, and the results they have achieved. This period of reflection is an important part of maximising and consolidating the learning from the *Acceleration* phase.

MEASURING SUCCESS
Participant looks at achievement against coaching outcomes.

The Measuring Success meeting also helps them prepare for their Sustaining Growth and 3-Way Final Review meetings, which kick off the next phase, *Continued Success*.

Chapter 9, Measure results, explains the Measuring Success meeting in more detail.

Continued Success phase

Continued Success

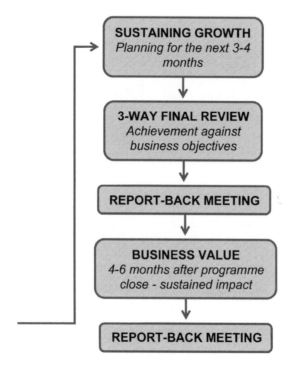

The *Continued Success* phase begins with a Sustaining Growth meeting. Participants consider how to maintain the gains they have made during the programme and how to continue to extend their growth over the next 3-4 months.

Chapter 9, Measure results, explains the Sustaining Growth meeting in more detail.

The 3-Way Final Review again facilitates effective communication between participants and their line manager. This is where they

> **SUSTAINING GROWTH**
> *Participant considers how to maintain and build on achievements.*

agree on what the programme has helped the participant achieve against business objectives.

As with the Progress Review, the 3-Way Final Review maximises the value of the coaching to participant, line manager,

> **3-WAY FINAL REVIEW**
> *Participant & line manager discuss achievement against business objectives.*

and client company, and is also useful for marketing purposes. It ensures that everyone fully understands and appreciates the difference our coaching has made. It primes them to become powerful advocates for our coaching, and provides material for success stories. With the client's consent, we use these success stories to promote our services inside and outside the client company.

Chapter 9, Measure results, explains the 3-Way Final Review meeting in more detail.

Following the 3-Way Final Review we always schedule a Buyer Report-Back meeting, where we

> **REPORT-BACK MEETING**
> *Coach meets the buyer to report on business value of participant's coaching programme.*

meet with the person who paid for the programme to discuss the value it brought to the business. Report-Back meetings are also where you can discuss further coaching opportunities with the buyer. Even if the buyer is the coaching participant or line manager, we always schedule a Report-Back, as it focuses on building the business-to-business rather than coaching relationship.

Chapter 10, Leverage the relationship, explains Report-Back meetings in more detail.

Then, 4-6 months down the line, we schedule a Business Value meeting with coaching participants to measure achievements since the close of their programme.

> **BUSINESS VALUE**
> *Coach meets participant to review Sustaining Growth plan and discuss longer term business value of the coaching programme.*

Chapter 9, Measure results, explains the Business Value meeting in more detail.

Again, following this meeting, we always schedule a Buyer Report-Back meeting, as before.

> **REPORT-BACK MEETING**
> *Coach meets the buyer to report on business value of participant's coaching programme.*

Chapter 10, Leverage the relationship, explains Report-Back meetings in more detail.

Make no mistake: Marketing and selling still requires hard work and dedication, but it's less stressful now that we have an integrated marketing and delivery process that plays to our strengths as coaches. Our process is streamlined, repeatable and successful!

Now that you've seen this overview of our leadership coaching marketing and delivery process, perhaps you can see why we live for process. Process is great!

However, you'll need more than a good process to succeed in your leadership coaching business. You'll need to be able to tell your potential clients what you do, what problems you solve, and whom you solve them for.

It's time to look at the value you bring.

Chapter 4: Focus on value

Show your alligator teeth

If your business is running a stand for tourists where you sell dream catchers and recordings of whales singing off the island of Maui, you can probably get away with marketing messages that are flowery and whimsical. *This is NOT the way to sell a professional service such as leadership coaching to Blue Chips.*

Even if you pitch them your services at the company picnic, you need to be DIRECT when dealing with Blue Chips. Their time and attention spans are short. Their eyes are on the prize. You need to tell these leaders what's in it for them and for their company. Otherwise, how will they know what value you bring? And if they don't know the value of your service, why should they consider paying for it?

Having the right marketing messages is essential for success in any business-to-business service. Blue Chips pay for services for one reason only: *to solve problems that have a negative impact on their business results.* It doesn't matter whether they're buying cleaning, recruitment, or consultancy on strategic planning, Blue Chips only pay for services they believe will help them improve how well and how fast they do what it takes toward achieving a net financial gain. If you can't convince them that your service will do just that, they won't buy.

To gain access to leaders in Blue Chips and make a success of your coaching business, you need to show your alligator teeth. When a leader asks you about your coaching, do you speak confidently about the difference it can make to them and to their business? Or do you disgorge a mass of information in hope that something tumbling about in there catches their interest? Do you cover your own confusion about the value you offer with sporadic nervous laughter? Do you present them with a mighty alligator or a quivering gerbil?

The marketing messages we used at Accelerated Success when we first started out were a garbled hotchpotch that managed to say everything and nothing, all at once. We would chuck in any available scrap of information in the hope that this would somehow encourage prospects to sign on the dotted line. Despite all that we threw at them, we made two giant omissions:

We neglected to tell them whom our service was for.

We neglected to tell them what they would get out of it.

After our big 'aha' moment, we finally understood that the purpose of our core marketing messages *wasn't to sell our services at all*. Leaders in Blue Chips don't commit thousands of pounds to buying a service after reading or hearing a brief statement. The best we could achieve with our marketing messages was to stir their interest enough to engage them in deeper conversation. And the best we could achieve from that conversation was to agree to a next step, perhaps to send them some information or schedule a follow-up call or meeting.

Our marketing messages only needed to say the right things to get us a second look from our target audience, leaders in Blue Chips. We then needed a clear idea of what to do next to move them closer to a sale.

Just to repeat, in case you got lost there: *The purpose of your marketing message is NOT to make a sale. It is to move one step closer, in a series of defined steps.*

Through research and testing (also known as 'trial and error'), we have discovered the marketing messages that speak to leaders in the correct way. Our messages now succeed in engaging Blue Chip leaders in conversations about our services, and gain real traction for us in moving toward winning business.

In our line of work — yours, too — marketing messages cannot afford to be unfocused. They must not confuse, bore or irritate leaders, or send them fantasising about their next holiday. Marketing messages like these quickly become part of the white noise of corporate life, and your potential clients will tune you out.

Always, always, always put the value of your service up front. The *ultimate* value, that is. By all means talk about the many areas where leadership coaching brings value, such as role transition, team building, driving change, raising performance, managing people and leading teams, but never forget the bottom line: *better business results*!

Value is about ultimate outcomes, not just the stuff along the way. Clearly stating the value you bring to your Blue Chip clients is vital for effective marketing.

Target, Problem, Outcome, Story

Knowing you need to clearly state the value you bring to your Blue Chip clients is one thing. Actually stating it is another.

Articulating the value of leadership coaching is difficult. It's tricky to say it in a way that people readily understand. There's a good chance that if you don't come up with the right wording, you'll give up and go back to what you were saying before. I mean, how important can it be?

Very important. If you can't define the value of your own coaching when you have a blank sheet of paper and oodles of time, how are you going to manage when you're in front of a potential client who has two minutes to spare?

There's no way around it — you have to do the hard yards in thinking about the value of your leadership coaching before you begin speaking to prospects. After that, every prospect you speak to is another opportunity to practise and retool as you start to say it in a way that is more clear, concise and compelling.

Describing the value of your service isn't a one-off. It's an ongoing organic activity that becomes habit as you improve your marketing and expand your business.

Having a good example for how to say it is enormously helpful. We learned the following very simple and powerful model for describing the value of a business service through Robert Middleton's Marketing Mastery programme (www.actionplan.com).

After seven years of zero growth Geraldine felt sure her marketing strategy would come good this time round

The first step is to come up with a value statement and accompanying client success story. You state clearly what your clients get out of working with you, and provide evidence of a particular client who got these results. Your value statement forms the basis of all your other marketing messages, although you can substitute different success stories.

Target	Leaders in Blue Chips with whom you want to work
Problem	The challenges they face and that you can help them overcome
Outcome	The business results leaders in Blue Chips want and that you can help them achieve with your leadership coaching
Story	The business results your existing and past clients have achieved with the help of your leadership coaching

Your **Target, Problem, Outcome** statement can be something along these lines:

We work with business leaders in complex and high-pressure roles. They know they could make a real difference if they worked more strategically, but are frustrated by the demands of operational issues and short-term business targets. They want to develop longer-term vision for their part of the business, reduce fire fighting, and maximise their contribution and that of their team for a step-change improvement in business results.

No frills, and it might not win a Pulitzer, but it states the value of what you do. Your potential clients are not left guessing, and you have a clear starting point for engaging in a marketing conversation where you can find out more about their situation and tell them more about your service.

This is where your success story comes in.

Once you have stirred the interest of a business leader with your value statement, you need to grab their full attention. They're busy people, so you'll need to substantiate your claim quickly or they'll move on. A deluge of random information about leadership coaching is more likely to leave them wishing they hadn't asked.

What they want is compelling evidence that backs up your claim. Few things are more compelling than a good story, so give them one of yours! Tell them about a leader you worked with and the business results your coaching helped that leader achieve — you'll find some of our success stories in this book, and if you want to see more, take a look at our website, www.acceleratedsuccess.co.uk, which is packed full of them.

Go to the source

Target, Problem, Outcome, then finish off with a Story. Sounds simple, right?

Actually, it can take forever to find the perfect way to describe the value of your leadership coaching. Are you happy with saying just 'leaders' for your target, or should you specify what *type* of leader? The list of problems they face is endless, so which ones should you use? Maybe you'll just skip over that for now and move on to the client story …

but which one? Hard to know until you're clear about the rest, so you go back and start over.

The thing is, you can't know the value of what you do simply because you're good at doing it. Only the client can know and experience the true value. A great way of identifying the problems your clients face and the outcomes you helped them achieve *is to ask them*.

Luckily, asking your clients what they got from working with you also provides you with the stories you can then use to illustrate your value statement. Wonderful! To top it off, this is a great way of reconnecting with past clients and can lead to further business if you manage it properly.

Chapter 6, Leave them wanting more, describes exactly how to win business by reconnecting with clients in this way.

At Accelerated Success, when we asked our clients what they got out of working with us, we were surprised and encouraged by how much difference we had made. We also got some great stories that demonstrate the value of our services.

For example, we worked with an IT consultant who managed an account with a global telecommunications company, and was heading for a showdown with a key client stakeholder. The relationship had deteriorated almost to a state of crisis. We helped the consultant identify strategies for pulling the situation back from the edge. His next meeting with the client went so well that he ended up selling them another £400K of services — far exceeding his original target, and positioning the account for a long-term, productive relationship.

We knew this client had got a lot out of his coaching, but we never realised until we asked him that he embodied such a powerful example of the value of our service. His coaching engagement finished before his £400K contract was signed, so if we hadn't asked him later, we might never have known.

You won't always get these gems where, as a direct result of working with you, your client can tell you the exact value of your service in pounds sterling. Still, we benefited so much from asking our clients what they got out of working with us that we decided to build it into our marketing and delivery process for every leadership coaching programme we delivered.

That's why at the end of every programme, we always have Measuring Success and 3-Way Final Review meetings, and then follow up with a Business Value meeting 4-6 months after programme close. These meetings add hugely to the value of our services for the coaching participant and client company, and are excellent for marketing purposes. Few things are more effective in selling further coaching programmes to existing client companies than helping them see what great results they got from previous programmes. We also use their success stories on our website to promote our services to other potential clients.

Focusing on value is good for you as a coach, and good for your clients. No question!

What and how to ask

To research content for your value statement and success stories, set up a few informal meetings with past clients to ask them what they got from working with you. They'll benefit from revisiting their learning and identifying the difference it has made, so there's also something in it for them. We've found that clients are very happy to help us in this way. They enjoy reconnecting, and they understand how it adds value for them, so don't be scared! Make a few calls to try it out for yourself.

You will need to make the purpose of the meeting clear:

> *I'm helping clients maximise the value of their coaching and gathering feedback to help me improve my services.*

You can send them your questions in advance to help them prepare. Then take them through these questions during the meeting, using your coaching skills to help them really think through their answers.

A good opening question is:

> *What is coaching for you?*

Having set them off thinking about their view of coaching, you can follow up by digging deeper:

> *What did you want to get from your coaching?*
> *In your opinion, how successful have you been in achieving the outcomes we set for your coaching?*
> *How did our coaching conversations translate to your work?*

You'll need to drill down and challenge them, an exercise that is tailor-made for a coach. You'll enjoy the exchange, and so will your client!

When drilling down, always ask what difference working with you has made to their business results — revenue, customer satisfaction, quality ratings, whatever performance indicators they use.

> *What impact did your coaching have on achieving your business objectives?*
>
> *What impact did it have on your team? Your line manager? The wider business? Customers?*
>
> *What evidence is there to demonstrate the impact of your coaching? What performance indicators were affected? What other ways can you see the impact?*

Their responses will vary. Only a few will be able to attribute specific improvements wholly to your coaching, but you will get compelling, credible and practical information about the value of your service anyway.

Remember, you are not looking for results that are exclusively tied to your coaching — although it's great when you get them. You are looking for results where your coaching provided the catalyst for change, where discussion during your sessions enabled participants to take action in the workplace that had a positive impact. And you want to know what that impact was, whether it was for the individual, the team, or the business as a whole.

Be realistic about your expectations. At the same time, avoid being overly modest. Your leadership coaching adds huge value. Be bold in identifying what that value is.

At the end of these meetings, ask clients if you can use the output for marketing purposes in the form of a success story. Assure them that the story will be anonymous, and that you will not use it without their approval.

Generally, clients are happy for their feedback to be used in this way, and enjoy their story being shared.

Get your story straight

Following all this research on the value you bring your clients, you can revisit the **Target, Problem, Outcome, Story** model to have another crack at writing your value statement and success story. Remember, updating your value statement will be an ongoing marketing activity for you, so don't put yourself under pressure by insisting on perfection right away. Produce a statement that you can use, and try it out with potential clients as soon as possible. Review how well it went every time you use it. Try pairing it with different stories to see which have the greatest effect.

The best stories tell of how ordinary people, just like you and me (or even a Blue Chip leader), battled against the odds, overcame adversity, and finally, triumphantly, succeeded. Stories feel real to us because we relate to the characters — we share their pain, aspirations and joy. Your stories will feel real to Blue Chip leaders because they'll recognize the people in them and the problems they face, and want the same outcomes for themselves.

Your success stories demonstrate the value of your leadership coaching in a clear and compelling way, but don't go overboard. Keep stories BRIEF and make sure they echo the **Target, Problem, Outcome** model:

Target	The hero, a hard-pressed Blue Chip leader
Problem	The challenges this person faced, and the heroic deeds that ensued
Outcome	A happy ending – business results such as improved levels of service, more satisfied customers, and increased revenue, profit and margin

If leaders you speak to as potential clients have similar problems, they'll connect with you and your service. Your story taps into their pain, and they'll see you as someone who understands their situation. You'll grab their undivided attention — at least for a brief moment. If they want outcomes similar to those in your story, you can engage them in conversation along those lines, asking them more about their situation, what they want to achieve, and the challenges they face. You can also give them further information about how your leadership coaching can help them.

Chapter 5, Turn leads into genuine prospects, gives more information on conducting this sort of marketing conversation.

On the other hand, if leaders you speak to as potential clients do NOT connect with the problems identified in your value statement and story, it's possible that your services are not a good fit at this time, and you can move on after a brief and pleasant chat. No pressure, no angst, and no chasing after someone who isn't a genuine prospect for your services.

Dare to target your ideal client

Targeting the right people is the first item in the **Target, Problem, Outcome, Story** model.

As a leadership coach you target leaders. Straight forward enough. Then again, maybe not. The word 'leader' can describe a large number of people in any business, large and small. You need to know what *type* of leader you want to do business with. You need to make this as clear as possible in your value statement and in your success story. If you don't, you'll end up taking on work you don't really want, or not getting any work at all.

A common, almost obligatory mistake we all seem to make with our marketing is to target too broad an audience. We try to be all things to all people in the unhelpful (nonsensical?) belief that targeting the widest market increases the number of potential clients.

It doesn't work this way. If your target market is basically anybody you can get in front of, your value statement and marketing messages will sound uninspiring, or even be a total turn-off:

We work with anyone who will pay us, whatever their problem, with various results.

It's easy to kid yourself that by not being too specific with your marketing messages you speak to a wide and varied audience. In reality, you don't speak to anyone. Marketing messages that are vague and all-inclusive do not grab attention — certainly not from the right people — and they are no good for selling leadership coaching, particularly the kind that guarantees repeat business from Blue Chips. Wailing at the moon would be a better strategy.

You will get far superior results when you dare to be highly focused with your marketing. The more precisely you can describe the leaders you work with, your **Target**, the more clearly you will be able to describe the **Problems** you help them with and the **Outcomes** they can expect. The more effectively you do this, the faster your target audience will recognize themselves in your marketing messages. They'll think, 'Hey, that could work for me', and they'll be prompted to engage in conversation about your services.

All you are doing by being less precise is rather half-heartedly offering yourself to a wider but much less interested, even totally *un*interested, group of leaders. Back to the corporate white noise problem, which is fine if your aim is to be ignored.

If your marketing is targeted, it improves your chances. If your marketing is vague, it reduces your chances.

Most people who run their own business totally get this concept. Even so, many of us cling to being vague because it somehow feels safer. We repeat the same pattern for failure in the desperate hope that next time it will succeed. It's as if we are caught in a 'yearning cycle', where we trap ourselves in an endless loop:

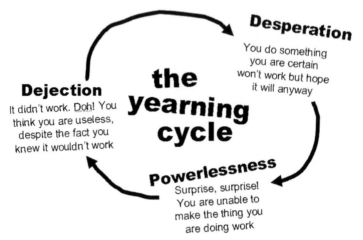

Desperation
You do something you are certain won't work but hope it will anyway

Dejection
It didn't work. Doh! You think you are useless, despite the fact you knew it wouldn't work

the yearning cycle

Powerlessness
Surprise, surprise! You are unable to make the thing you are doing work

At Accelerated Success, it wasn't until we plucked up the courage to switch our marketing strategy from yearning to learning that we were able to properly identify who we wanted to work with. Before this, we weren't specific because we didn't want to risk excluding anyone.

Desperation! Powerlessness! Dejection!

We finally broke out of the yearning cycle and decided to target the type of leaders we *liked* working with, the ones who benefit most from our coaching. We also decided not to waste time and effort on leaders who didn't fit the profile we had developed. We figured that it's best to sell to the leaders we work with best, so we thought we'd better clearly identify who those leaders were. Nothing personal, just good marketing sense!

So, who are these leaders we like to work with?

> *Our target leaders work in, or head up, rapidly growing regional offices of global ICT companies. Globally, their strategy is to grow both organically and through acquisition. They have a strong sales focus and commitment to high levels of technical excellence and customer service. They value learning on the job and look to nurture talent and leadership within the company. They take calculated risks on innovative leadership development solutions, and they leverage those results.*

> *The leaders we work with demonstrate a drive for success and a desire to make a difference and deliver beyond expectations. They have a strong commitment to their own learning and growth. Their values are well aligned with those of their company. They have a willingness to challenge norms, take risks and execute plans. They are key players in achieving business objectives.*

At Accelerated Success, we are clear what type of leaders are our ideal client, and what type of company they work for. This makes it much easier to develop marketing material to engage them, which in turn helps us do business with them and then win further business from their companies.

It's up to you to decide who the right people and the right companies are for you. If you ask past clients what they got from working with you, you'll be clear about the type of leader and company where you got the best results and with whom you most enjoyed working. You'll also get a feel for the type of leader and company where you do less well or are less happy.

All you need to do *now* is to write up target leader and company profiles. You're not after a vague notion of who or what they are. You need to be absolutely clear in your mind so you can genuinely target them, not just cast around for anyone who'll give you the time of day.

Your **target leader profile** describes the type of leader you want to work with and for whom your coaching can make the most difference. Include professional ambitions, values, attitudes, interests, lifestyle, etc. (psychographics) along with age, income level, how many and what kind staff they manage, and also gender, race and ethnicity if relevant (demographics).

Your **target company profile** describes the sort of company your target leaders work for — such as company mission, philosophy, management style, reputation in the industry sector, commitment to learning, how entrepreneurial, etc. Also, facts and stats on industry sector, number of employees, annual revenue, location, customers, and who you sell to in the company.

In these profiles, describe whatever you think will be useful in identifying and winning your ideal client. You don't have to decide it all in one sitting, but once you have profiles that describe the 'right leaders' and 'right companies', you can pitch your marketing messages accordingly.

Doesn't that feel better? You don't need to approach everyone you see on the street in a suit. You can step away from panic-driven marketing, and use your existing contacts to target the leaders and companies you actually want to work with. Phew!

Now that you know what value you bring and for whom, it's time to use that knowledge to get in front of potential clients and engage them in a marketing conversation.

Chapter 5: Turn leads into genuine prospects

Boo!

There's an old sitcom routine in which two single people meet on a blind a date. One of them, desperate for a lasting relationship, and despite all advice to keep the conversation light, can't help blurting out the history of previous failed relationships and how much they want marriage and children. It's too much, too soon, and there's no second date.

Even if you're nervous during your first meeting with a potential client, don't ask them to marry you or buy a coaching programme before you've even shared a coffee. You'll scare them away! You want to come across as a highly competent and confident professional, not someone who is desperate and prone to panic.

Your aim with the first conversation with a potential client is to find out whether there's value for both of you in scheduling a second conversation. Ask about their work situation. Give them some information about your services. You're certainly not at the stage where you should be trying to walk down the aisle or sell them anything.

At Accelerated Success, we generate new leads from our existing clients and contacts, so the 'second date' is usually a Strategy Session (don't worry, we'll be covering those in the next chapter). If we generated leads via networking, it would take a bit more time and effort to move things along, and our success rate might be reduced. We've used both approaches, so believe us when we say that our current approach is much more effective!

Now, when a potential client agrees to a Strategy Session, we know we've converted that lead into a genuine prospect — we're already at the second date, the next step of the process. If the potential client doesn't take us up on our offer, we check out whether it's a straight 'no, not interested, thanks', in which case we can part comfortably on good terms, or whether it's a 'yes, I'm interested, but this isn't the right time', in which case we agree on a date when we'll be back in touch.

Our simple aim with a potential client in the early stages of the relationship is to get them to agree to a free Strategy Session. That's all. We're not trying to sell a full coaching programme or reserve a hall for the wedding reception. We set up a Strategy Session because it is the key tool we use for converting prospects to paying clients. We deliver these sessions for all genuine prospects, whether we've connected with them through identifying further business opportunities with an existing client, perhaps their boss or human resources department, or via referral by an existing or past client.

Send them something!

Imagine this scenario. You're meeting a potential client. Where do you start? What do you do?

Send them something!

If you were dating, you might send a box of chocolates or a dozen roses or a humorous cat video from YouTube. Blue Chip leaders do not take kindly to such entreaties so send them something they'll find useful: an article that describes in a compelling way the results your previous clients obtained from working with you. The article, an important weapon in your arsenal of marketing currency, can focus on value as well as describing some of the features and process of what you do. Mainly, it needs to be *short*, easy to read, and genuinely interesting or even exciting to your prospect. An article gives you an appropriate excuse to ask for their contact details so you can send it to them. If you're attempting to set up a meeting, you can attach the article as a PDF file to the email in which you suggest dates. If you've already agreed to a meeting, attach the article to your email confirming time and venue.

What's that you say? You don't have an article handy that presents your services in an exciting and compelling way?

Write one!

We know that sounds like a tall order, but if you can't write it on your own, pay a professional to help you or even write it for you. It only needs to be a few pages, and you've already done the hard work of crafting your value statement, much of which you can repurpose. It's worth the initial effort or expense, because this article helps potential clients get a real understanding of what you do and the results you get. Just the act of writing it helps you develop a deeper understanding of your vision for your business.

In addition to sending your exciting and compelling article, you can send general information about your services — structure, methodology, case studies, whatever you think they might actually want to read. Not too much though! Don't send an encyclopaedia, starting with Volume A-H. It needs to be easy to skim and digest.

This is where having a decent website is also useful. Your website doesn't have to be huge, just enough pages to contain information that would interest potential clients — who you work with, the problems they face, the outcomes they're looking for, and success stories from your past clients. **Target, Problem, Outcome, Story**. Include something about the structure of your coaching programmes, and perhaps offer your article for download. *Don't post content to your website unless it has a marketing purpose.*

Have THEM do the talking

When you find yourself in a marketing conversation, don't panic! It's tempting to start hurling all sorts of information at your potential client, but that's rather like bumping into someone you hardly know at the station and delivering a diatribe on all your health issues, family concerns, and lifetime disappointments. If you dump a load of trash, there's not much in the conversation for them. Certainly if a prospect asks about your services, you should respond, but don't use it as an opportunity to chuck the kitchen sink at them. Better to send them something prior to or after the meeting, such as your article and a link to your website. During the meeting itself, just focus on the value of your leadership coaching by steering the conversation that way.

How? Good question! The answer is to *stop trying so hard to tell them stuff*. TMI (Too Much Information) can feel like another unwelcome complication in the life of a busy leader. Adding to their list puts more pressure on them — not a good way to get them fully engaged in understanding the value of what you do.

Ironically, to present yourself as a solution and not another complication, *do as little talking as possible*.

That's right — be a coach! Get *them* to do the talking. Ask them about their situation, their vision for their business, and the challenges they face. Get them to tell you what's important to them and what's hurting them in their work. Connect with their pain and allow them to immerse you in their preoccupations. *Be the solution*, the one that unburdens them. Get them to tell you about their role, their problems, and the outcomes they want.

Get them to tell you their story.

When they've done all this, THEN you can tell them a bit about your services.

Let the jury be quite clear! Asking a senior manager about their work situation to pass the time of day is not illegal. However, to do so for marketing purposes is a loathsome act and a criminal offence.

If they are genuinely potential clients for you, then by telling you about their situation they will better connect with what you have told them about the value of your leadership coaching services. They'll work out for themselves that YOU might be the solution they are looking for. The value of your services suddenly becomes tangible, because they can apply it to their specific situation — it moves from being a story about someone else to being about *them*.

An added bonus of this approach is that they see you as a good listener who provides them with the space to get things off their chest and have insights. Use your coaching skills to help them make the connection between their situation and your value statement. When prospects fail to make that connection, it is an indication they do not need or want your services, at least not at this time. (Or sometimes it's an indication that you need to work a bit harder to win them over.) As they describe their situation you will be clearer as to whether they are the right match for you, so you can prioritise prospects and focus on the most likely candidates.

The way to present your services as a solution is by letting them talk about their problems, not burying them with information before they're ready or can properly understand it.

Create leads without stress

Winning further business from existing or past clients is always a good idea for leadership coaching businesses. It's also a relatively low-pressure way to practice the art of the follow-up.

The best opportunities — the low-hanging fruit — are where existing or past clients are the decision makers and budget holders, and where the new opportunity is to give them further coaching or to coach a leader who reports to them. Go for this first! You have a very good chance of success by following a few simple steps.

Perhaps the existing client is a director you have previously coached. Arrange a brief catch-up meeting or call to further discuss coaching needs across their business. You can make the initial contact by email.

> *Hi Christine,*
>
> *I know you're going through your planning cycle for next year. This might be a good time to meet and review your vision and the challenges you see ahead, and to discuss if I can be of further help.*
>
> *I can make a 30-minute call any time on Wed 15 June, Fri 17 June, or Tues 21 June, or I am happy to schedule a call at a time and date of your choosing. Let me know what works for you.*
>
> *Regards*

Word the email to suit your style, but keep it brief and to the point. Always offer up to three times and dates. This makes it easier for your client to say yes, and to reply quickly. If you don't offer dates you are leaving it for them to sort out, which adds to their list of things to do, which makes it a burden even if they want to say yes.

Also, when it's on someone else's To-Do list, it may never get done.

If you have delivered value to your client and have built up a good relationship, you've earned the right to ask for this meeting. This might sound overly bold, but it's true! If your service really makes their life easier, they will give you their time.

You just have to ask for it.

Offer them something of value — time to think and talk out loud. During the meeting, ask them about their situation, their short- and long-term objectives, their challenges, their plans for achieving these objectives, who the key players are on their team, etc. *Do not try to sell them anything*. Instead, share with them your stories of where you have helped other clients who faced similar challenges.

At this stage they may be thinking about further coaching for themselves. If they aren't sure, you can suggest a Strategy Session to help them with their decision. Or perhaps they'll name one or more on their management team who might benefit from and be interested in coaching. Where this is the case, use your coaching skills to help them think things through.

You don't have to coach them to an actual decision at this stage. Instead, suggest a Strategy Session as a next step:

Would you like me to contact this person and offer them a Strategy Session to help them focus on their vision and challenges? They will be able to decide whether coaching would be useful for them, and I can report back to you with a recommendation.

The director is very likely to say yes. Our clients generally do. They've experienced our Strategy Sessions and full coaching programmes, and they are fully aware of how it has helped them and added value to their business. In the above scenario, the team member benefits whether or not there's additional coaching, and the director gets help in planning and decision-making.

Making the decision to cultivate further business in this way from existing clients is not a tough one. You've delivered great results for them in the past. All you're doing is arranging a conversation to see if you can do more of the same in the future. Now you've taken care of the low-hanging fruit.

Well, not quite. There's often more to be had if you want it. You can arrange similar meetings to ask existing clients for referrals to colleagues in other parts of their business and contacts outside their business. Many coaches think of actively seeking referrals as being overly pushy, but it doesn't have to be awkward for either side when managed correctly.

Once existing clients have introduced you to potential new ones, you can contact these new leads the same way as above, with a few variations. The aim is still to set up a

Strategy Session. The leaders to whom you have been referred get something of real value for free, for which they will thank the person who made the referral.

Chapter 10, Leverage the relationship, gives more information about how to manage asking for and following up on referrals, as well as further information on cultivating business from existing clients.

The key to the universe

There is one way you can GUARANTEE significant improvement in converting leads to genuine prospects, and it does not depend on the way in which you generate your leads. Are you ready for us to reveal the big secret? Are you sitting down?

ALWAYS, ALWAYS, ALWAYS follow up!

The reason for this is screamingly obvious: By following up, you are actively continuing the relationship. By NOT following up, you are passively ending the relationship. You can sit there and hope your leads will contact you, but it's pretty certain they won't. They've got so many other things on the go, you won't be anywhere near the top of their list.

This does not necessarily mean they're not interested. They might have forgotten about you. They might have wanted to call but never got around to it. Why should they, when they can quite rightly expect that YOU will call THEM?

It's your business to follow up. The other person may be annoyed if you don't.

If you're anything like we used to be at Accelerated Success, even when you absolutely know you should follow up, you kind of … *don't*. Following up is not something you particularly enjoy, so you talk yourself out of it. *They'll think I'm bothering them.*

You put it off for a day or two. *I don't want to seem too desperate.*

You tell yourself you're too busy. *I'm too busy.*

You might even resort to more convoluted thinking. *Yes, I suppose in many ways they're my ideal client, with whom I could build a long and productive relationship, but I'm just not sure they're quite the right fit for me.*

Do not sabotage your chances of success. Follow up!

When you DO finally follow up, perhaps after much procrastination and unhelpful internal dialogue about how they will greet your advances with the same enthusiasm they would news of a rail strike, be absolutely clear about the purpose of your follow-up. Even if you just send a short email, know what you want to achieve with that email. At some stage you'll need to speak by telephone, so know what you want to achieve by the end of that call before you make it. We've gone as far as having a template for these types of calls, with scripts that help us take the stress and uncertainty out of the conversation and ensure that we get to the point and don't waste anyone's time.

Remember, you are not aiming to sell them a coaching programme in the early stages of the relationship. It isn't

going to happen. Just be clear on the outcome you want when you follow up.

Chapter 6: Leave them wanting more

Winning business with Strategy Sessions

At Accelerated Success we delivered a Strategy Session for a vice president in a global ICT firm. He was relatively new to his role, and had been working flat out, focusing on achieving quarterly and annual revenue targets, and learning his leadership role on the job. This was the first time he'd stepped back and thought about his longer-term vision for his part of the business. He got so much out of his Strategy Session — taking the time to think more strategically about where he wanted to take the business and how to get there — he asked us to conduct similar sessions with each member of his management team. Following all these sessions, we reported back to the VP with recommendations for individual tailored coaching programmes for him and his team.

It was a lot of work up front for us, but the VP went on to commission Accelerated Success programmes for him and several of his team — *more than 40K worth of business from one initial Strategy Session with one business leader*.

Since then we have made Strategy Sessions central to our marketing. Sure, they are time consuming, but they are really no more work than the marketing activity we used to do. Because the sessions are so targeted, we wind up spending more time with fewer — but far better — prospects. In turn, they win us a lot of future business.

Also, these sessions are enjoyable and rewarding to deliver. What's not to like?

Strategy Sessions provide a natural and dynamic progression from focusing on value with your marketing. Through them, you help prospective clients dig down into the problems they face and the outcomes they want. You can then tell them about the value of your leadership coaching, that it helps leaders like them overcome the same kind of problems and achieve similar outcomes. You cannot do this with the right amount of credibility if you are not clear yourself on the value of your service, the problems your clients face, and the outcomes you can help them achieve — so you see how using this as a marketing tool always comes back to absolutely knowing the value you bring.

Although we've given you a way of identifying the value of your services in the *Focus on value* chapter, from experience we know it isn't as easy as it sounds, and is always a work in progress. You can get stuck here, unable to nail down your value and therefore unable to move forward with Strategy Sessions.

Fortunately, there is a way you can learn how to deliver these sessions even before you have fully articulated your value statement:

Why not ask past or existing clients to help you try out a new leadership-coaching tool free of charge?

You can explain that by participating they will get a clearer understanding of how they can add most value in their role, and that it will help you gain the practical experience of using this approach.

Learning to conduct Strategy Sessions this way does not put the same pressure on you as in a live marketing situation. You might even win new business from it!

Getting started with Strategy Sessions

That's how we started using Strategy Sessions at Accelerated Success. We asked a small number of existing clients if they would help us road test a new leadership-coaching tool. We got practice using Strategy Sessions, and it helped us think about the sort of leaders we wanted to work with and the wording of our value statement. An unexpected benefit of this exercise was that we even won some business! One of the leaders we worked with got so much value out of this 'practice' session, he commissioned a full leadership-coaching programme for himself.

Strategy Sessions really are that powerful! They bring real value to participants, giving them an experience of your leadership coaching and leaving them wanting more. Following that early success, we won a lot of further business from the same client company. The Strategy Session didn't just help us sell one leadership-coaching programme, it helped us initiate a long-term and highly productive business relationship.

As you can imagine, we have put a lot of effort into understanding how and why these Strategy Sessions are so effective. We have rigorously researched, tested and refined our approach to them. We now use Strategy Sessions to help us cultivate further business from existing clients, either coaching them or the leaders who report to them. We also use them to pursue referrals to contacts in the same or other companies.

When we meet with existing clients to cultivate further business, we ask who else on their team might benefit from our coaching, and suggest a Strategy Session for anyone they identify. After delivering the sessions, we report back to the original clients. This method also helps them in planning and decision making around leadership development — they know our coaching makes a real and positive difference to business results, and Strategy Sessions are a great way of helping them see where else in their business they can use it.

When cultivating business from existing clients in this way:

o **Over 90 percent of leaders** to whom we offered a Strategy Session accepted.

o Of these, **over 90 percent said yes** to a full coaching programme for themselves and / or members of their team.

Where we think existing clients can refer us to one or more of their colleagues, we ask them to make the introduction via an email that briefly explains the value our leadership coaching has brought to their business. We follow up and arrange a first contact meeting, at which we offer potential clients a Strategy Session as a next step.

With **referrals from existing clients to colleagues** in other parts of the same company:

o **Over 50 percent accepted** our offer of a Strategy Session
o Of those who accepted, **over 90 percent commissioned** a full coaching programme for themselves and / or members of their team

With **referrals from existing clients to contacts in other companies,** we target only a few in any one year. So far, **100 percent of the external referrals we have targeted have accepted a Strategy Session**. Of those, one in three has become a long-term client.

Proactively seeking and converting referrals is discussed in more detail in Chapter 10, Leverage the relationship.

Reconnecting with existing contacts to offer Strategy Sessions is a convenient entry point to our marketing and delivery process. You can also use Strategy Sessions with new contacts. However, it makes sense to make the most of the contacts you already have. At Accelerated Success, we offer these sessions as the norm to both new and existing contacts who fit our target leader and company profiles.

Take another look at chapter 5, Turn leads into genuine prospects, to see how we do it.

Now that you have used your marketing messages to promote coaching that is targeted at helping leaders achieve business goals as a valuable solution for Blue Chips, your Strategy Session is designed to keep the momentum going. It needs to live up to the billing that this type of coaching enables leaders to drive change, transform organisations, delight customers, and significantly improve business results. Your prospect should leave the Strategy Session firmly convinced that leadership coaching is of huge value to Blue Chips — which, of course, it is. A slide presentation, an information sheet, or a run-of-the-mill meeting is not going to be enough.

The Strategy Session is a startlingly good marketing tool. As an experienced coach, you are remarkably well equipped to deliver it, because it is actually a highly focused coaching session. With practice, and as you deepen your understanding of the true value of your service and what type of leaders leverage it best, you will be delivering these high-value sessions only for prospects you think you can genuinely help and that you actually want to work with. You will then be able to convert most of these prospects into paying clients — certainly more than half of them, and probably more than 90 percent. Have you ever read or heard about a marketing technique that you wanted to try more?

Strategy sessions enable prospects to focus on what can really make a difference to them and their business, and will give them first-hand experience of the value of

your service. **They will view your leadership coaching as the solution they've been looking for, and will leave wanting more. This won't just happen because you turn up at their offices. You need to prepare yourself and your prospects properly prior to the meeting. You then need to deliver a tightly focused, high-value session. Finally, it is essential to report back on the session, to underscore and maximise its value to your prospects, and to provide a natural point at the end of the Report-Back to engage them in a sales conversation.**

Preparation
Delivery
Report

Preparing for Strategy Sessions

In preparation for a Strategy Session, send your prospect brief information about the purpose and structure of the session and about your leadership coaching services. (If you have an article or information sheet, send one or both.) The crucial bit of currency to send them at this point is a preparatory questionnaire that they complete and return to you prior to the session. It should take them 20-30 minutes to complete. Completing the questionnaire helps them think in detail about their business vision, and the challenges they face and what they need to get better at to achieve it. Reading their responses also enables you, the coach, to understand more about their situation and plan how to deliver the session. Without this questionnaire, you risk wasting a lot of time in the session itself gathering information, rather than drilling down and enabling participants to gain genuine insight and understanding about their business.

Other advantages of using a pre-session questionnaire are that it takes the pressure off both of you in the Strategy Session — participants know a bit about what to expect, and you have more control over how the session unfolds. It also shows that you know what you're doing — you have a clear and professional process that they can engage with, reducing any anxieties they might have and helping to build trust.

The questionnaire we use at Accelerated Success is as follows:

1. What's the purpose of your part of the business?
2. Describe how you fit into the organisation, including who you report to, the size of your team, and budget / revenue generation responsibilities.
3. What's your vision for your part of the business?
4. What are your key objectives for the next 12-18 months?
5. What are the 3 or 4 most important and challenging areas of your role in fully achieving these objectives?

6.   What would it be most important for you to get better at, to significantly improve performance in these areas? Try to select something that will extend your capability as a leader / key player, rather than something technical you can accomplish by learning a new skill.

You can adapt these questions to your own situation and style, or develop your own questions entirely. For example, we use slightly different questionnaires depending on whether leaders are considering coaching for themselves or leaders who report to them. Sometimes you won't know this information at this early stage, in which case the Strategy Session is where you will find out.

Experimenting with different questions will help you see what works best. The important thing is to elicit information from participants that will enable you to quickly enter into a high-value discussion about their work situation during the session itself. From the responses they give in the pre-session questionnaire, you will also be able to decide what supplementary questions to ask during the session that will enable them to thoroughly explore their situation.

Delivering Strategy Sessions

Successful delivery of the Strategy Session is easier when you get the preparation stage right. Once in the meeting, after the usual introductory chitchat, thank prospects for completing and returning the questionnaire. Give them a copy of the session agenda and briefly talk them through it:

o   Purpose of Strategy Session
o   Working through your completed questionnaire
o   About my coaching services
o   Your questions
o   Schedule Report-Back

Remind prospects of the purpose of the Strategy Session, which is to provide them with the opportunity to look at their vision and challenges in their role, and what they need to get better at to achieve their vision.

Tell them that everything you discuss will be kept confidential. If you will be reporting back on the session to their line manager, let participants know that you will send them their written report for approval before sharing it with the named individual. Ideally when reporting back to a line manager, make the Report-Back a 3-way meeting, involving the participant also. This is a very effective way of removing any concerns around confidentiality, and enhances the value of the Strategy Session to participants and their line manager. It encourages greater and earlier buy-in from both, and keeps the sales process moving along.

Let participants know you will be taking notes on the discussion to write up in their Strategy Session report. If you want to digitally record the session, first check that they are comfortable with this and explain that it is to help you recall content for writing the report. Tell them that you will explain more about your leadership coaching services following the main discussion. Finally, ask if they have any questions before you get started.

Ask the right questions

Now comes the bit where you should be the most comfortable and confident. It's coaching!

Explain that you want to go through their responses from the questionnaire and ask them further questions to really understand their work situation. Get them to explain in more detail what they mean in each of their written responses. If you are not recording the session, take notes as you go for putting together the Strategy Session report.

The questionnaire and supplementary questions are in the Strategy Session Quick Guide in The Alligator's Dance section of this book.

As an experienced coach you will know when to dig and when to move on to the next question. You are not trying to elicit wonderful insights (although these will likely come at some stage). You are simply giving them the opportunity to explore their work situation in detail — where they want to be, the challenges they face, and what they need to get better at to overcome their challenges.

At question 6 you will dig deepest. This is where the power of the Strategy Session truly lies. The issues identified here will become the focus for any future coaching programme. First get them to connect with their PAIN in their role. Help them identify the stuff that hurts most, the seemingly intractable problems connected with their work challenges. You can help participants by discussing each problem area in turn:

6. What would it be most important for you to get better at, to significantly improve performance in these areas? Try to select something that will extend your capability as a leader / key player, rather than something technical you can accomplish by learning a new skill.

    What's the one area, that if you made significant gains here, it would be a big deal for you personally and add value to the business?

    How do you know this is a problem?

    If you don't get better in this area, what happens? And then what happens? And what does that affect?

Drill into their responses to gather evidence about the extent of each problem area for them and for their business. This is their opportunity to really understand the problems they face, how much they are hurting, and how much they want to fix them.

Then you can ask participants what they want instead. Help them connect with the GAIN of sorting out their problems. What it will feel like when they get to where they want to go, and the value of doing so to them, the people around them and their business.

    What would getting better in this area allow you to do, which you can't do today?

    Where do the benefits of being able to do this show up?

    What will it allow the business to do, which it can't do today?

Now help them get specific about the value of making change.

> *What's the value of addressing this area?*
>
> *What is the ultimate gain for you? Your team? Your line manager? The wider business? Your customers?*

Don't be put off if participants find this tough — they probably will, which is why it's worth doing. Encourage them to take a good look at the value of overcoming their challenges in their role. Help them connect with the difference it will make for them and for their business. It is likely participants will describe the value of overcoming their challenges as a combination of better results and less aggravation and stress. Help them dig deep here, to understand and describe the value. Not only will this be useful to them, it's great for your marketing purposes too. It will help participants see your leadership coaching is about improving their work situation and business results.

Closing the Strategy Session

Keep to your agenda. You must leave time to tell prospects more about your leadership coaching services. Not TOO much more, but they will need to know something about what your coaching can help them achieve, and the structure and timing of a coaching programme. You also need to deal with their questions and discuss any limitations or concerns they have about participating in a full coaching programme. For example, most will want to know how much such a programme will cost, if they haven't already asked. Be as clear as you can, and don't start offering a discount before you've even got their reaction to the price. A helpful approach for them and for you is to give a range:

> *The cost depends on the type and duration of the coaching programme you take. I will be able to recommend which programme would be best for you once I have written up your Strategy Session report. For leaders in similar situations, it costs from [£ lower end figure] to [£ higher end figure]. How does that sound to you?*

If your price range doesn't coincide with the sort of money the participant is prepared or expecting to pay, now is the time to find out. No point in spending time trying to sell your services to someone who is definitely not going to commission a full programme. However, more often than not, because Strategy Sessions help them focus on the value your programmes can bring to their business, the cost is not the crunch issue it might have been. If the session goes well, participants will already know whether a full programme is a good solution for them. In this circumstance they need to know cost to help them make it happen.

Any discussion about cost is also a useful point for you to find out about their buying process. Your marketing job is made easier when either the participant or their line manager is also the decision maker / budget holder. Where this is not the case, you need to find out who holds the purse strings and how you can help move the decision making process along. These can feel like tough conversations, but it's best to be direct.

Some useful questions:

What is the buying process?

What do you need to do to get to a decision?

Is there anything I can do to help you move things along?

Finally, always schedule the Report-Back session before you close the Strategy Session. As mentioned previously, where possible make the Report-Back a 3-way meeting involving the participant, their line manager and you. This may not always be possible but, where it is, it helps you get buy-in from and build relationships with the key stakeholders in the coaching programme, and establish clear lines of communication. This maximises your chances of selling a full programme.

Reporting back

The report you produce following the Strategy Session is a summary of what prospects say during the session, a couple of pages at most. The purpose of the report is to provide them with an understanding of their work situation and what they want to achieve, which they can read through and reflect on. You can attach to this your recommendation on which of your leadership coaching programmes is most appropriate for them, along with more information and pricing for the recommended programme.

The report is not in any way an analysis of what was said, or of their personality, or their professional strengths and weaknesses. You cannot produce that sort of analysis with validity or credibility from a Strategy Session, and you don't need to. The value of the Strategy Session is to give the participant the opportunity to think and talk in depth about their work situation while someone else listens attentively and neutrally. The value of the report, therefore, is to give them an opportunity to further reflect on what they said. It's a simple yet powerful approach. They often get very energised by their Strategy Session Report-Back. It helps them see addressing and overcoming their challenges as something real and attainable, and they see the coach who delivered the session as someone who listens and really understands them. You are now a professional they can trust and with whom they would like to work.

There is also clear value in the Report-Back for line managers. At any one time they are likely to be considering a number of options for developing leaders in their part of the business. If you and the participant can show in the Report-Back meeting what your leadership coaching can bring to the business, you are helping the line manager with their planning and decision making. If the line manager is also the budget holder, they will be clearer on what they will get if they spend part of that budget on your services. If they are not the budget holder, they will have compelling evidence they can present to whoever is, to influence the decision to buy your services.

Your chances of a sale are further increased if any other leadership development options under consideration don't demonstrate the value they bring as powerfully as you do.

The value of the Strategy Session Report-Back to you and your leadership coaching business becomes very clear. You demonstrate the business value of your services to the key stakeholders in the buying process, the potential participant in a leadership-coaching programme, the line manager, and the person who holds the purse strings if different. You help them understand the participant's challenges and the value of overcoming them. You connect the challenges they have and the outcomes they want with the outcomes you have helped leaders in similar situations achieve. They see your leadership coaching as a solution that can help them achieve their business objectives. You've made a credible and compelling case for the budget holder to buy your services.

That's what you want from your marketing!

You can use whatever format suits you best for the report. At Accelerated Success we tailor each report to individual situations. For example, when a participant has key insights during their Strategy Session, we headline the information at the top of the report to make it easier for the reader to understand. This is not an attempt to make certain information more prominent as a way of manipulating potential clients into buying our services! Yes, you want to avoid half-baked analysis and trite conclusions, but you also want to present the information in an accessible and compelling way.

Let's assume you have set up a 3-way Report-Back meeting with the participant and their line manager. Here are some useful questions to ask the two of them in this ideal scenario:

> *Have you read the report?*
>
> *Have you had time to meet and review the report together?*
>
> *What is your response?*

Coach participant and line manager through this conversation and give them time to answer your questions in full.

Some useful questions to ask participants alone:

> *Where are you with your thinking since our Strategy Session?*
>
> *What did you get out of reflecting on your vision and challenges?*
>
> *What is your sense about participating in a full coaching programme?*

Some useful questions to ask line managers:

> *What are your thoughts on commissioning a full coaching programme?*
>
> *What has to happen next for us to move forward?*

The sales conversation happens at the end of the Strategy Session Report-Back. If you think your leadership coaching will help participants overcome their challenges and achieve their vision, say so. Refer them to the recommendation you made in the report and tell them briefly about other leaders you have worked with in similar situations, and the results they got. After you've done that comes the moment when you have to square up to what is the scary bit for most leadership coaches — *you have to ask them if they want to buy, and they have to decide yes or no.* If you keep it simple, it isn't half as bad as you might think. Ask them:

Are you in a position to make a decision now?

It's worth noting here that decision making in Blue Chips follows various routes. Sometimes it's quick, but sometimes it's frustratingly slow. When it's slow it might simply be about having to go through an administrative process, which can take time even with green lights blazing. Other times it can seem to take forever because the decision that affects you is a relatively low priority in a complex and high-pressure environment. The decision itself may take a matter of minutes, but it can take a lot longer for them to get around to addressing it.

Of course, it could be something else entirely. When it comes to Blue Chips, there are a thousand and one things that can delay such a decision. During this time, your job is to do what you can to move things along — keeping in touch with the line manager and participant by phone, offering to speak to others in the organisation on their behalf to explain your services, asking whether testimonials from other clients will help, sending them any further information they need.

Your job here does not include getting hung up on why there's a delay. We are all capable of snatching defeat from the jaws of victory by listening too attentively to our internal monologues doubting the value of our services, our credibility and our worthiness. Realistically, you'll have a very good idea of the participant's level of interest from how their Strategy Session went. And you'll have a very good idea of the line manager's interest from the Report-Back. If you think they're genuinely interested, just accept that these decisions can take time in Blue Chips. Don't take it personally, and don't give up on a good prospect through lack of confidence or not knowing what to do next.

When you finally win the business, all the data generated by the Strategy Session becomes invaluable. You use it to help participants identify outcomes to work toward during their coaching programme, and those outcomes are aligned to achieving their business objectives.

Chapter 7: Align with business objectives

Align it to win

Spare a thought for today's Blue Chip leaders. It's not easy for them. Pulled in all directions, leaders can feel they are reeling from a barrage of heavy blows, rather than driving business success.

They strive to make a real difference to their business but too many things get in the way. Short-term demands and targets hustle vision and strategy off to the sidelines. Operational issues and sorting out other people's problems steal their time. They feel bullied into reacting to situations beyond their control rather than proactively moving forward with their own agenda. They rarely get the chance to focus on what they see as the high-value activity in their role. When they do, it's difficult for them to know where to start. Even then, they barely have time to gather their thoughts before they get dragged into the next crisis.

The flip side is that when Blue Chip leaders get things right, they can transform organisations and significantly improve business results — which is where you come in. Leadership coaching that is properly aligned to achieving business objectives enables Blue Chip leaders to deliver better results, faster, with increased job satisfaction and less stress. Aligned coaching helps leaders connect what they do in their role with the bigger picture, enabling them to focus on what they need to get better at to maximise their contribution to big-picture results for their company.

Aligned coaching aims high, has a clear purpose, and is measurable. Coaching that isn't aligned with achieving business objectives doesn't pack the same punch. If you don't target big-picture results, you can't expect to get them. You may be adding value, but great results are only achieved by taking on the big challenges.

On top of this, if you don't align with business objectives, you can't explain the difference your leadership coaching makes in terms of business results. This makes it much harder for your client to properly understand the value you bring, which makes it harder for you to win further business with them and through their referrals.

Benefits of aligned leadership coaching

What you get	Aligned	Non-aligned
Big picture	Yes	*Maybe*
Defined purpose	Yes	*Not really*
Measurable	Yes	*Difficult*
Clear value	Yes	*Unlikely*
Good marketing	Yes	**No**

Aligning leadership coaching with business objectives works for your clients and it works for you. It's also what Blue Chips want, according to the 2012 learning and development survey undertaken by the Chartered Institute of Personnel and Development (CIPD)[2]. Nearly half of all respondents to the survey of private and public sector and non-profit organizations anticipated over the next two years greater integration between coaching, organisational development and performance management to drive organisational change. This indicates a significant trend in Blue Chips is to connect individual coaching and performance with the bigger picture.[1]

It makes sense, therefore, to target your coaching at helping participants achieve their most challenging business objectives. This is where you can make the most difference for your Blue Chip clients, and it enables you to measure the difference you make. This is also where you get your success stories, which help you win more business.

Getting alignment right enables participants to leverage their coaching to achieve the best possible results. *Alignment* is the first of the three phases of our leadership coaching marketing and delivery process, introduced in the *Lead the way* chapter. The diagram from that chapter is repeated below, with the *Alignment* phase highlighted.

---

1 Chartered Institute of Personnel and Development (CIPD), Annual Survey Report 2012, Learning and Talent Development. CIPD is the world's largest Chartered HR and development professional body, with over 135,000 members across 120 countries.

ACCELERATED SUCCESS PROCESS

Alignment

STRATEGY SESSION
Vision & challenges

REPORT-BACK MEETING

3-WAY START UP
Links to business objectives

OUTCOME SETTING
Agreeing targets for the participant's Accelerated Success programme

Acceleration

ACCELERATED SUCCESS SESSIONS
Regular meetings and/or calls for discussion, learning & planning

Execution

Review & reflection

3-WAY PROGRESS REVIEW
Session to review progress against outcomes

Realignment

MEASURING SUCCESS
Achievement against outcomes

Continued Success

SUSTAINING GROWTH
Planning for the next 3-4 months

3-WAY FINAL REVIEW
Achievement against business objectives

REPORT-BACK MEETING

BUSINESS VALUE
4-6 months after programme close - sustained impact

REPORT-BACK MEETING

The diagram below is a close-up of the *Alignment* phase from the previous diagram.

Alignment

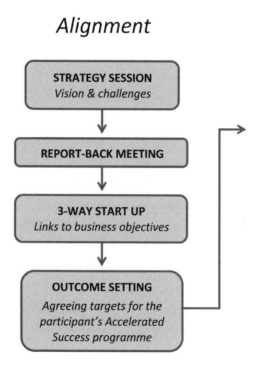

Adding the bite

You learned all about Strategy Sessions in Chapter 6, *Leave them wanting more*. Here's some more to help you put real bite into those sessions.

In addition to being a powerful marketing tool, the Strategy Session provides the crucial first step in aligning a coaching programme with business objectives. It helps participants connect what they do with the bigger picture, and identify the key challenges in achieving their business objectives. The Strategy Session report then becomes a working document to which participants refer throughout their coaching programme.

In our experience, participants achieve far more through their coaching by taking on challenges one at a time, in order of importance. It enables them to take significant leaps forward on each one. These leaps represent great achievement in themselves, but can also significantly change the business landscape for participants. Challenges that once seemed important gradually become less so, or even dwindle into non-issues. Ultimate outcomes can therefore be very different and far more stretching than originally anticipated.

But this can only happen by taking on challenges one at a time and then reassessing.

They start by identifying their challenges during the Strategy Session. At the start of their programme they identify a single coaching outcome, then work toward it for the first 3-4 months of their programme. Once they have achieved this outcome we refer again to their initial report, compare their achievements against their first outcome, and identify the second most important challenge.

We worked with the leader of a consulting team who wanted to improve team performance — better responsiveness and service to clients, less fire fighting and blame throwing, and increased sales and revenue. She started by focusing on clarifying and clearly communicating her business vision to everyone on her team. As a result, people were more open and trusting, communicated more effectively, and enjoyed their work more. Their increased engagement led to significant improvement in team performance.

Our client was surprised. She had originally intended to follow up by getting tough with them. Now she didn't have to. That helped the client see her situation in a new and more helpful way. The crucial factor in raising team performance rested on her leadership. The next outcome she worked toward in her coaching programme was aimed at improving planning and objective setting across the team, and managing workflow to enable them to hit short- and long-term targets. This was one of the challenges listed in her Strategy Session report, but she hadn't expected to tackle it so soon.

The Strategy Session report ensures that all challenges are recorded and nothing is lost. As a coaching programme progresses, participants can use it to see how far they've come, and help them plan what to take on next.

3-Way Start Up

The 3-Way Start Up meeting between coaching participant, line manager and coach helps get everyone on board. It allows line managers to give their perspective on the challenge participants have decided to take on first, and to agree on how overcoming this challenge will have an impact on business objectives. This and further 3-Way meetings at the *Acceleration* and *Continued Success* phases of the coaching programme ensure that effective communication around performance is achieved throughout. This communication is essential to maintaining alignment and leveraging the success of the coaching.

A spin-off benefit of the 3-Way Start Up meeting is that it models best-practice-in-performance discussions between participant and line manager. Many of the leaders we work with find these discussions challenging even if they think they manage them well. Others don't feel they manage performance discussions effectively, and some admit to avoiding them whenever possible. When we facilitate effective performance discussions between participant and line manager in a coaching programme, both get valuable practice and a positive experience that stays with them and that they can transfer to other situations in the future.

To prepare for the 3-Way Start Up, we send participants and their line managers a briefing on what to expect. We also send participants a worksheet to return prior to the meeting. The worksheet reminds participants that at their Strategy Session they identified and discussed the one area, that if they made significant gains here, it would be a big deal for them personally and add value to the business. The questions we use in the worksheet are:

1. Assuming you make progress in this area, what can you reasonably expect to see changing over the next 3-4 months?

2. How will you know if you are making progress or not?
3. What ways could you measure progress in this area? Brainstorm and make a list. Think about quantitative indicators such as targets, margin, time spent on important tasks and customer feedback. Also think about qualitative indicators such as levels of stress, job satisfaction, collaboration and morale.
4. How will making progress help you achieve your business objectives?
5. How will working on this area extend your capability as a leader?

These and supplementary questions are in the 3-Way Start Up Quick Guide in The Alligator's Dance section of this book.

At the 3-Way Start Up meeting itself, it's a good idea to spend 15 minutes with participants on their own before the line manager joins them. You can use this slot to run through administrative issues for their coaching programme, such as terms and conditions for working together, confidentiality, coaching code of ethics, cancellations policy, and programme start and end dates and structure. You can also address any questions.

Enter the line manager. Now you can get straight into the real purpose of the meeting: The participant outlines the first challenge to work on and gets the line manager's views. The challenge is not going to come as a thunderbolt-from-the-sky surprise to the line manager, having already been at the participant's Strategy Session Report-Back.

Again, when you facilitate the 3-Way Start Up meeting, do what you do best: Use simple but direct questions to the participant and line manager. Taking each question in the worksheet in turn, you invite the participant to:

Tell us more about this.

Then, you can ask the line manager:

What's your view on this?

Coach both participant and line manager to share their views and develop a common understanding of the issues they are discussing. In particular, when discussing how participants will measure progress and the impact on their business objectives, useful questions for the line manager are:

Are these indicators of progress appropriate? Are they within [the participant's] *sphere of influence? Are* [participant's name] *12 month targets realistic?*

How do you think [participant's name] *business objectives will be impacted?*

At the end of the 3-Way Start Up, thank line managers for their input.

It's not rocket science. There's no form filling. You're just engaging coaching participants and their line managers in a discussion about the participant's performance. When done effectively, the 3-Way Start Up can add hugely to what participants achieve through their coaching, and in their role outside their coaching programme.

Note: These meetings can be difficult to schedule, given how inevitably busy everyone is. However, our clients tell us that they benefit a great deal from the 3-Way Start Up, so don't be tempted to skip this step.

Outcome Setting

Ideally, the Outcome Setting meeting between you and the coaching participant should take place immediately following the 3-Way Start Up. Here, participants nail down the outcome they want in tackling their most important business challenge. By this time, having completed a Strategy Session questionnaire, a Strategy Session and Report-Back, and the 3-Way Start Up worksheet and meeting, they usually know what they want. Your job as the coach is to make sure the outcome they settle on is clear, concise and measurable. You can start with:

> *We've discussed the one area, that if you made significant gains here, it would be a big deal for you personally and add value to the business.*
>
> *Now we need to identify an outcome for you to work towards in the first 3-4 months of your coaching programme. In three or four sentences, summarise the outcome you want in addressing this area.*
>
> *Make sure your sentences are stated positively — tell me what you want, rather than what you don't want. We'll work on the wording together, so don't worry about getting it right the first time.*

Outcome setting is all about helping participants think in detail about what they want to achieve through their coaching. As with previous meetings, this is not a highly technical process. It's *coaching*! Help them come up with an outcome they're happy with, one that makes sense based on all the thinking, discussion and learning they've done up to this point.

Once participants have clearly stated the outcome they want from tackling their main challenge, you can move them on to how to measure it. This is not new to them. They have thought this through when completing the worksheet in preparation for their 3-Way Start Up, and then discussed with their line manager at that meeting measurements and impact on business objectives. All they are doing here is finalising what they are already familiar with.

> *Based on our previous discussions, how will you measure achievement against this outcome?*
>
> *What will be the impact on your business objectives?*

Don't be concerned that this is too much repetition. You are covering the same ground but this is the first time participants actually nail down the measures they will use against their clearly stated outcome. They summarise and refine what has gone before. We find that participants value this opportunity to take stock and clarify their thinking. In addition, taking the time to get their first coaching outcome and measures properly articulated is essential in maximising the value of their coaching.

Once participants have achieved their first outcome from their most important challenge, they can agree to a second challenge and a second outcome. After that, a third, and so on. As they go along, their choices and outcomes are shaped and informed by discussions and achievements throughout their coaching programme. As they achieve against each outcome, they will very likely need to realign their thinking in light of the changes they make to their work situation.

Case Study: Celine

What does it actually look like to align coaching outcomes with business objectives?

The following case study is based on clients we have worked with at Accelerated Success. Celine is head of consulting in the EMEA region of a global ICT company.

The objectives

Celine has a number of detailed and challenging business objectives. Here is a brief summary of the main ones:

o   Achieve all financial targets for the year, including revenue of $110 million

o   Achieve all customer service level targets for the year

o   Expand the team by 75 people this year

o   Take over lead of support services division, realign it and grow revenues by 35 percent this year and 35 percent next year

o   Work with the new offshore service centre manager who reports to me, and get him up and running and hitting target this year

The challenges

During her Strategy Session, prior to her commissioning a full coaching programme, Celine identified the following as her most significant challenges:

o   *Recruiting the right calibre of people in such a short time frame — we just can't find enough of the right people to fill the posts.*
o   *I don't have any time to focus on the important things. I get dragged into operational issues and I'm **not making progress on the big stuff**.*
o   *The new offshore centre is having a negative effect on my team, who are worried about the impact on them, not knowing if their jobs are safe. Productivity is falling off.*

During her Strategy Session and subsequent 3-Way Start Up meeting with her line manager, Celine identified the following areas where she needed to raise her game:

o   ***I need to take the time to focus on the strategic.*** *At the moment I'm a bottleneck – the team comes to me with problems and expects me to sort them out. These are bright people and I know they could work out some of these issues themselves. I need to get better at delegating and trusting the team to deliver.*
o   *If I had more time I could think about how we address our recruitment challenges.*

o   *I need to keep staff motivated during this difficult time. Reassure them that the new offshore centre will not mean job losses or fewer opportunities.*

Celine was able to see that raising her game in the area listed above in bold — **I need to take the time to focus on the strategic** — was crucial to overcoming one of her main challenges, **not making progress on the big stuff**. She could also see that overcoming this challenge would help with the other ones. This understanding, and subsequent discussion with her line manager in her 3-Way Start Up, helped Celine decide which challenge she should take on first through her coaching.

During her 3-Way Start Up, Celine agreed with her line manager that the FIRST and MOST IMPORTANT challenge for her to focus on for the next 3 or 4 months of her coaching programme was:

o   *I don't have any time to focus on the important things. I get dragged into operational issues and I'm not making progress on the big stuff.*

The outcome

In her Outcome Setting meeting Celine produced a statement of the outcome she wanted in tackling her most important challenge. The coaching outcome Celine produced used language that meant something to her. She would be able to refer to it during her coaching to check progress and refocus her effort. Her coaching outcome included measures of success, which were linked to her business objectives.

Celine's coaching outcome for the first 3-4 months of her programme:

o *I want more time to think about and execute on the strategic initiatives I have to get done this year. I want the team to start taking responsibility for thinking about problems before they come to me, and come to me with ideas and options, not just problems. I want them to step up and take responsibility for executing once we've agreed on a way forward, and just keep me informed of progress.*

Alignment with business objectives

During her Outcome Setting meeting Celine identified how she would measure success against her coaching outcome and the business objectives this would help her achieve. She decided achieving her outcome through coaching would have a positive impact on all her main business objectives but one (expand the team by 75 people this year).

Her success measures were:

o **I will have more time to focus on the big stuff** — *I can diary this in and see how many hours I get here.*
o **I will feel less stressed** — *I'll be able to judge this for myself.*

o **My manager will be more confident that I'm on top of the strategic stuff and let me get on with it** — *I can ask for his feedback on this.*

o **The team will be coming to me with ideas about how to resolve problems** — *I will see how often they do this versus the times I just get problems.*

o **The team will be meeting without me to discuss problems and generate options for solutions** — *I will see how often this happens.*

o **Customer issues will be resolved more quickly and we'll have fewer escalations** — *this will show up in service level stats.*

o **There will be fewer arguments internally about our performance** — *I can get feedback on this in management meetings.*

o **Customer satisfaction will increase** — *this will show up in customer survey results.*

o **We must continue to hit quarterly and annual financial targets overall, and achieve increases in specific areas, as stated in business objectives** — *just because we're changing how we work, we can't take our eye of the ball with the financials. The financial reports will show how well we're doing.*

Chapter 8: Accelerate success

Coach the way you've always coached

We're not here to tell you how to coach. As an experienced coach, you know that already. So far we've explained how you can use your coaching skills to win business with leaders in Blue Chips and align your coaching to achieving business objectives. Now, at the *Acceleration* phase of our marketing and delivery process, you will use those same skills to coach as you've always coached.

You coach your participant against the outcome they identified at *Alignment*, to help them achieve their business objectives. They may work on this outcome for the entirety of their coaching programme, or they may complete this outcome sooner. If they do, once they have achieved the first outcome, you help them identify the next outcome and deliver against that, and so on. Each new outcome-setting discussion is informed by what came before, so that they are continually building on what they have already learned and experienced.

Acceleration is the second of the three phases of our leadership coaching marketing and delivery process. The diagram below shows the whole process, with the *Acceleration* phase highlighted:

.

135

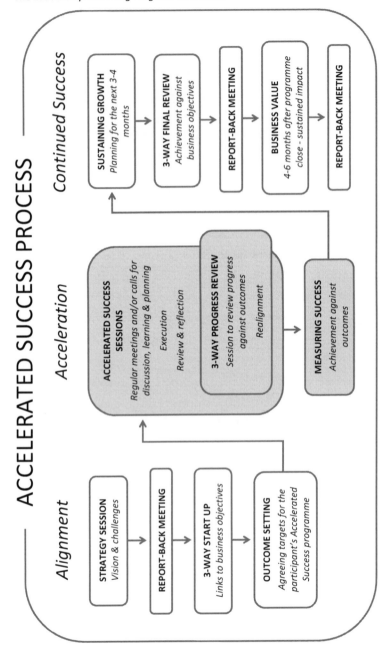

ACCELERATED SUCCESS PROCESS

Alignment

STRATEGY SESSION
Vision & challenges

REPORT-BACK MEETING

3-WAY START UP
Links to business objectives

OUTCOME SETTING
Agreeing targets for the participant's Accelerated Success programme

Acceleration

ACCELERATED SUCCESS SESSIONS
Regular meetings and/or calls for discussion, learning & planning

Execution

Review & reflection

3-WAY PROGRESS REVIEW
Session to review progress against outcomes

Realignment

MEASURING SUCCESS
Achievement against outcomes

Continued Success

SUSTAINING GROWTH
Planning for the next 3-4 months

3-WAY FINAL REVIEW
Achievement against business objectives

REPORT-BACK MEETING

BUSINESS VALUE
4-6 months after programme close - sustained impact

REPORT-BACK MEETING

The diagram below is a close-up of the *Acceleration* phase from the previous diagram.

Acceleration

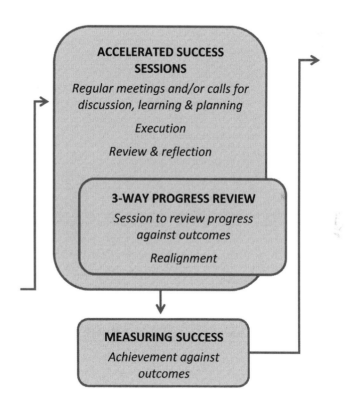

The table below shows the structure and a breakdown of hours for our Accelerated Success coaching programmes, the bit of our Accelerated Success Process we charge our clients for. Programmes run from **3-Way Start Up** through **3-**

Way Final Review. Depending on need, we usually deliver either a 7 or 10 month programme. They both include six hours of fixed-agenda meetings in the form of 3-Way meetings, Outcome Setting, Measuring Success and Sustaining Growth, plus either 9 or 15 hours of coaching against outcomes, delivered via face-to-face meetings, calls, or a combination of both. Outcome setting after the initial Outcome Setting meeting is included in the 'coaching' hours in the table.

The Accelerated Success programme:

Table showing structure and breakdown of hours for 7 and 10 month Accelerated Success coaching programmes

Sessions	7 month programme (hours)	10 month programme (hours)
3-Way Start Up	1	1
Outcome setting	1	1
Coaching	5	8
3-Way Progress Review	1	1
Coaching	4	7
Measuring success	1	1
Sustaining Growth	1	1
3-Way Final Review	1	1
Total programme hours	**15**	**21**

Although our clients get a lot of value out of the steps in our Accelerated Success Process that come before and after those in the table above, we do not charge for them. Our pay-back comes from new business these pre- and post-programme meetings enable us to win, either with the existing client or via referral to others in their company or to other companies.

Prior to an Accelerated Success programme start therefore, we always complete a Strategy Session and follow up with a Report-Back meeting. After programme close, we always complete the Report-Back meeting on the 3-Way Final Review. And 4-6 months down the line, we always complete Business Value meetings and the Report-Back on these. Basically, we always complete the full Accelerated Success Process. It's good for our clients and good for us.

Maintain alignment

It is not wholly unheard of in the Blue Chip world for individuals or teams to spend large amounts of time developing, refining and finalising plans, and then move on without even a glance at the fruits of their labours. Intricate and innovative blueprints for change gather dust on shelves or clutter up hard drives. Leaders and the people they lead are left to get where they need to go without the benefit of a roadmap. *Blue Chips get caught up in DOING and forget to refer to the PLAN for the doing.*

We all do this in some form or other. Have you ever stood in front of an audience to give a presentation you've been preparing for weeks, only to deliver the whole thing without once looking at your notes? Ever wound up having a totally different conversation with a prospect or at a meeting than you planned? It might be nerves, excitement, or lack of technique, but when you don't execute according to plan, it's harder to achieve what you want.

It happens. But it must not happen during a leadership-coaching programme!

You have to keep leaders focused and moving forward if you want to help them accelerate their success. *Be aligned, stay aligned, and plan and execute with real purpose.* It doesn't matter how well you align with business objectives at the start of a coaching programme if you don't enable participants to maintain and build on that alignment throughout their programme.

Maintaining alignment is a natural part of the conversation at the start of a coaching session:

> *What have you done since our last session?*
> *What do you want to focus on in today's session?*
> *How does that fit in with where you're trying to get to?*

It takes more than this, though, to leverage alignment and help leaders make a real and lasting difference. The 3-Way Progress Review at approximately the middle of a coaching programme is a vital tool in maintaining alignment. It facilitates discussion between coaching participants and line managers on what participants have achieved against outcome(s) so far and on the impact this has had on business objectives, and enables them to realign and focus for the next part of their coaching programme.

3-Way Progress Review

The 3-Way Progress Review allows participants to report back to their line manager on their achievements against their coaching outcomes and business objectives. It also allows the line manager to give their perspective on the participant's coaching. In this way, the 3-Way Progress Review helps maintain effective communication between participant and line manager around the participant's performance. It assists with maintaining alignment and maximises the value of the coaching programme to participant, line manager, and the business as a whole.

For the 3-Way Progress Review, as for the 3-Way Start Up, we send participants and their line managers a briefing on what to expect. We also send participants a worksheet for them to return prior to the meeting, asking them to think about their achievements so far against their coaching outcomes and measures, and what kind of impact this has had on their business objectives.

Your role as coach in the meeting is to facilitate an effective discussion around performance against coaching outcomes and how this connects with business objectives. It's easy here to let them digress into a general discussion about business issues that are not connected to the coaching programme. Keep them focused!

The worksheet questions and supplementary questions are in the 3-Way Progress Review Quick Guide in The Alligator's Dance section of this book.

A final note on notes

So far, we haven't suggested anything controversial or radical when it comes to maintaining and maximising the value of alignment. It's an integral part of the coaching conversation and can be enhanced by a 3-Way Progress Review. Great stuff! The real big hitter, though, is to keep a decent coaching record.

The coaching record provides a dynamic for change. It enables participants to stay focused on high value activity, shows them how far they've come during their coaching programme, and helps them plan how to sustain their growth once the programme is finished.

At Accelerated Success, our coaching records contain at minimum:

o   Participant's completed Strategy Session questionnaire and report
o   Required outcomes for the Accelerated Success programme, as identified by participants following discussion with their line manager, and what kind of impact these outcomes will have on business objectives
o   Clear and concise notes on each coaching session

Not all leadership coaches use coaching notes. Some are adamant that they *won't* use them. At Accelerated Success, we firmly believe that clear and concise coaching notes play an essential part in maximising the coaching participant's success. Without them, both coach and participant waste time at the beginning of each session trying to remember what was covered last time.

These notes record all the key information from the session and form part of the coaching record. They also leverage the value of each session and the programme as a whole. Clear and concise notes are an essential 'aide memoir' for both coach and participant prior to each session, and can be used to track achievement against agreed-upon actions. They provide focus for 3-Way review meetings.

Our coaching notes do not constitute a verbatim transcript. They simply record the participant's key thoughts, insights and planned actions for each coaching session — 200-300 words in total. Any more than this can be unusable.

For us, not taking coaching session notes just doesn't make sense. We believe you cannot do without them. Which brings us to the question: Who should take these notes — participant or coach?

One view is that participants will take greater ownership of action plans coming out of their coaching if they take the notes themselves.

We disagree. We only work with leaders who are fully committed to driving change for improved business results. If they aren't, it becomes clear at their Strategy Session, if not before, and we don't take them on as clients; to do so wouldn't be good for them or their business, or for our business and us. Whether participants take their own notes during sessions, therefore, shouldn't make any difference to their ownership or level of commitment.

On the other hand, because coaching notes are pivotal to the value of our programmes, we make the *coach* responsible for taking them, typing them into the coaching record, and sending the updated record to participants within 48 hours. In this way we ensure the programme delivers the best possible results — good for clients, good for us. This is part of the service, and we factor it into our pricing.

Chapter 9: Measure results

Bring meaning to measure

Measure results!

Easy to say, but there are several schools of thought on how to do this when it comes to leadership coaching. Some people don't think it's actually possible. However, if you want to sell leadership coaching to Blue Chips, you need to be able to provide evidence of the difference it makes to individual leaders and the business results they achieve. Without this sort of evidence, the alligator of your leadership coaching is still trapped in the business backwaters, and you'd be denying Blue Chips a powerful tool for change and growth, as well as holding your business back.

At Accelerated Success, we believe that the evidence you provide about the value of your service must be genuinely meaningful to clients and potential clients. Sounds obvious, but it's very easy to get it wrong here. What's meaningful to *you* might not be as meaningful to *them*, and there's no point presenting them with information they can't readily relate to and understand, or that lacks credibility.

We have found that the best way to generate meaningful evidence about the value of our services is to support clients in doing the measuring themselves.

We don't do it for them. We get them to look at the difference our coaching has made for them and for their business. We have already helped them identify the coaching outcomes they want, and how to connect those outcomes with their business objectives. At the close of their programme, we facilitate effective communication between participants and line managers around how well the participant has done, and we close the *Acceleration* phase of our marketing and delivery process with a Measuring Success meeting with the coaching participant. From there, we move into the *Continued Success* phase with a Sustaining Growth meeting and the 3-Way Final Review.

We use Measuring Success, Sustaining Growth and 3-Way Final Review meetings to provide a structure for measuring results. Via these meetings, we support participants and their line managers in understanding what has been achieved against business objectives, and to what extent coaching played a role in getting there. This is a performance discussion, the kind that is the norm around individual and business performance.

Measuring results in this way helps everyone quickly relate to the evidence around the participant's performance and results, and it's in a language they use regarding issues they connect with. They are therefore readily able to deepen their understanding of the issues through discussion. The conclusions they arrive at have high credibility with them because they get there themselves.

Liza's coaching had enabled Henry to mend the hole in his bucket, that much he was sure of. How this helped him in his role as operations director of a global software solutions company was not so clear to him.

This brings us full circle to *Focus on value*. Ask your clients what value your service has brought to their business. In doing so, you further increase the value you bring. Coaching participants and their line managers understand what was learned, the changes that have been made, and the results achieved. This additional learning helps participants sustain improvement and transfers their learning to new challenges going forward. It also helps line managers appreciate the value of your leadership coaching, which helps them with planning and decision making around future coaching programmes for themselves and leaders in their patch.

If you are not getting your clients to fully engage with measuring the results they achieve through your coaching, you are seriously decreasing the value you bring.

Measuring Success

The final meeting of the *Acceleration* phase of our marketing and delivery process is the Measuring Success meeting. This is an opportunity for coaching participants to look back over everything they have achieved through their programme. It's valuable learning for them, and usually highly motivating. Often they are surprised at how far they've come, which reinforces their success and gives them a sense of satisfaction at making a difference.

The Measuring Success meeting is the first of two meetings, the second being Sustaining Growth, which together help participants prepare for their 3-Way Final Review. We have found that participants are energised by this part of their coaching programme. Most will put a great deal of work into reviewing their achievements and planning their next steps. Some have developed slide presentations for showcasing their achievements at their 3-Way Final Review.

Participants are familiar with the territory by now. At the start and during their programme they have identified outcomes and measures, and links to business objectives. They have also been through a 3-Way Progress Review, where they looked at how well they were doing against outcomes and objectives. They are therefore well prepared to measure their success, building on what has gone before.

As always, to maximise the value of the Measuring Success meeting, we send participants a preparatory worksheet. The worksheet asks them to refer to their Strategy Session report, the coaching outcomes and measures they agreed to during their programme, and their coaching notes. It then asks them a series of questions that will help them articulate their achievements over the course of their coaching programme:

1. To what extent have you fully achieved your outcome(s)? Rate yourself on a scale of 1-10, where 10 is fully achieved and 1 is the opposite.
2. What have you done that has helped you achieve your outcome(s)? Think about specific actions / initiatives you have taken, practices you have put in place, and behaviours or new approaches you have adopted.
3. Looking at the indicators you identified for measuring achievement towards your outcome(s), where are you against these indicators now? Refer to your coaching record to help you here.

4. Where were you against these indicators when you began your coaching programme? Refer to your coaching record to help you here.

5. What other evidence is there to demonstrate your achievement towards your outcome(s)? Think about what is happening differently. Also think about how your team, your line manager, others in the business and customers would answer this question.

6. How has working towards your outcome(s) helped you achieve your business objectives?

7. How has achieving against your outcome(s) helped you extend your capability as a leader? Think of specific examples.

At the start of the Measuring Success meeting you can remind participants that this discussion will prepare them to present their achievements to their line manager. This will help them consider their answers in a way that is meaningful to them and to their boss.

To stimulate discussion here you can use simple phrases such as:

Tell me more about this.

Ask suitable questions to drill deeper where you need to. Look for examples of where the challenges participants have been working on have changed. Help them uncover examples of new practices they have put in place, new behaviours they are using, and insights into their own style and approach. Then you can move on to making the connection to their achievements against business objectives.

You are not necessarily looking for results that are wholly and definitively attributable to your leadership coaching (although it's great when you get them!). You are looking for results where your coaching provided the catalyst for change, where discussion during coaching sessions enabled participants to take action in their workplace that had a positive impact — and you want to know what that impact was, whether it was better results for the individual, the team, or the business as a whole. Given that participants know that what they say will later be shared with their line manager, they will want to get into detail to be sure they can substantiate their achievements with hard evidence.

The worksheet questions and supplementary questions are in the Measuring Success Quick Guide in The Alligator's Dance section of this book.

Sustaining Growth

The Sustaining Growth meeting moves us to the *Continued Success* phase of our marketing and delivery process. *Continued Success* is the third and last phase of our leadership coaching marketing and delivery process. The diagram below shows the whole process, with the *Continued Success* phase highlighted.

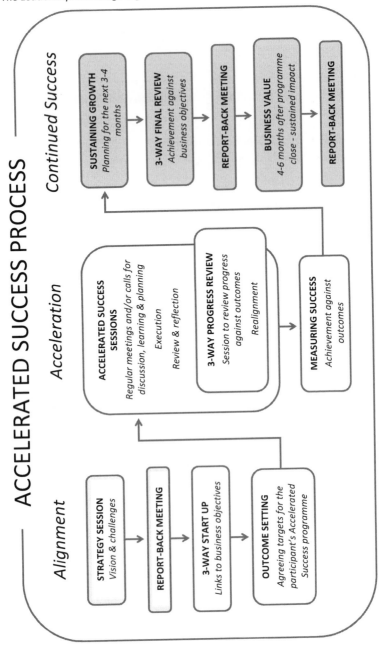

ACCELERATED SUCCESS PROCESS

Alignment

STRATEGY SESSION
Vision & challenges

→

REPORT-BACK MEETING

→

3-WAY START UP
Links to business objectives

→

OUTCOME SETTING
Agreeing targets for the participant's Accelerated Success programme

Acceleration

ACCELERATED SUCCESS SESSIONS
Regular meetings and/or calls for discussion, learning & planning

Execution

Review & reflection

3-WAY PROGRESS REVIEW
Session to review progress against outcomes

Realignment

→

MEASURING SUCCESS
Achievement against outcomes

Continued Success

SUSTAINING GROWTH
Planning for the next 3-4 months

→

3-WAY FINAL REVIEW
Achievement against business objectives

→

REPORT-BACK MEETING

→

BUSINESS VALUE
4-6 months after programme close - sustained impact

→

REPORT-BACK MEETING

The diagram below is a close-up of the *Continued Success* phase from the previous diagram.

Continued Success

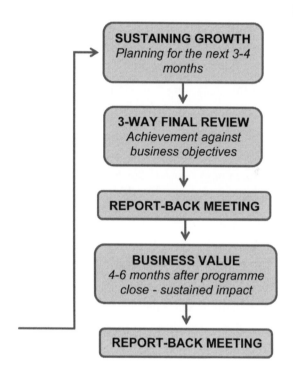

Now that the Measuring Success meeting has helped participants look back at and measure their achievements, the Sustaining Growth meeting helps them look 3-4 months beyond the close of their programme, and to how the gains they have made can become business as usual. This helps them transition back to working life without a coach, and forms part of their preparation for the 3-Way Final Review.

We have found that this 3-4 month horizon is perfect at this stage; anything longer than that is hard to come to grips with. During the Sustaining Growth meeting, the coach helps participants to develop their thinking around their responses in the preparatory worksheet.

The worksheet questions and supplementary questions are in the Sustaining Growth Quick Guide in The Alligator's Dance section of this book.

3-Way Final Review

The 3-Way Final Review is where participants tell their line manager what they have achieved through their coaching programme, what impact this has had on business objectives, and how they plan to sustain their gains over the next 3-4 months so that change sticks. Participants use output from their Measuring Success and Sustaining Growth meetings to prepare and showcase their achievements.

Line managers also have an important role to play. The 3-Way Final Review is their opportunity to assess the participant's claims to improved performance and the impact on results. They can also give their perspective on what they have seen changing throughout the duration of the coaching programme.

Your role as coach is to facilitate an effective discussion around the participant's performance. As with all 3-Way meetings, you can brief everyone on their role in the meeting, and you will have participants complete a preparatory worksheet.

All three of you will be familiar with the format of a 3-Way meeting by now, having previously conducted 3-Way Start Up and Progress Review meetings. However, you may have to work hard to keep everyone on track. It's easy for them to digress to unrelated side issues, so keep them focused.

With this meeting, you are helping everyone drill down to measures of what had been achieved through coaching. You're not trying to introduce anything new here. The questions in the 3-Way Final Review worksheet are a combination of those used in the Measuring Success and Sustaining Growth worksheets and meetings. The difference is that this time, participants answer them for the benefit of their line manager.

The worksheet questions and supplementary questions are in the 3-Way Final Review Quick Guide in The Alligator's Dance section of this book.

Take each question in turn and ask the participant to:

Tell us more about this.

After each time the participant has finished ask the line manager:

What's your view on this?

It is likely that you will be able to facilitate a free-flowing discussion, using questions to steer it. Again, the most challenging part for the coach is keeping the conversation on track. You have helped the participant generate more data about performance than can be covered in this short meeting, so help them prioritise by asking about the most important achievement or most impactful. You want to make sure you cover the entire agenda for the meeting so that all parties get value from the session. Keep notes of what's said, and type them up into the coaching programme final report.

As at the 3-Way Progress Review, line managers will often express surprise at what they hear in this meeting. They may not have been aware of how many improvements in the business were down to the coaching participant, or that participants had targeted the improvements that were made as part of their coaching programme.

Participants like the 3-Way Final Review because they get the recognition they deserve. Line managers like them because it lets them know what's going on in their patch and whom they can rely on. These meetings are great for facilitating effective communication around performance.

At the end of the meeting, thank everyone and explain that you will write up the coaching programme report based on the discussion you've just had. Tell them you will provide each of them with a copy and will schedule a Report-Back meeting with the buyer, the person who has paid for the coaching programme. If this is the line manager, you can schedule the meeting now. Explain that the Report-Back meeting is an opportunity to look at the value coaching brings the business and where else they might use it.

Before you close the meeting, explain that you will contact the participant in 4-6 months to carry out a Business Value assessment.

Business Value

The Business Value meeting takes place 4-6 months after programme close. The coach helps participants to measure the impact their coaching has had further down the line. They review how well they have done against their Sustaining Growth Plan, and what their coaching programme has helped them achieve in the longer term.

This is the real test of any coaching programme — has it made a significant and lasting difference?

For participants, Business Value meetings are a way of revisiting previous successes and refocusing and energising their efforts going forward.

For coaches, these meetings provide an opportunity for you to reconnect with participants. In addition, you can reconnect with line managers (and buyers if different) by scheduling a Business Value Report-Back meeting with them.

Through Business Value and Report-Back meetings participants and line managers / buyers gain an increased understanding of the value of your coaching to their business. This is a great time to ask them about further business. Far from being forced or awkward, it's a very natural next step. It would feel like a very odd omission to all involved if you didn't ask clients where else in their business you might help them. It's all part of the service you offer.

More on this in Chapter 10, Leverage the relationship.

Quantitative AND qualitative

Aligning and measuring leadership coaching in this way isn't some lame attempt to present qualitative data in pseudo-quantitative terms. It's a way of enabling Blue Chip clients to readily engage with and fully understand the impact of the coaching on business results. It is both quantitative and qualitative, and your clients will find it compelling and credible because they do the measuring and analysing themselves.

Don't be fazed by thinking that Blue Chips only want quantitative data. Certainly, they like it — so measure and present your leadership coaching results in this way where you can. However, think back to the *Focus on value* chapter and the power of the *Target, Problem, Outcome, Story* model for developing marketing messages. Stories are a great way of presenting both quantitative and qualitative data that can grab the attention of leaders in Blue Chips and be the starting point in helping them understand the real value of leadership coaching to their business. Don't imagine, therefore, that Blue Chips won't also value qualitative data about the impact of your service. Both quantitative and qualitative data are valuable, despite the bad press the latter sometimes gets.

The bad press is understandable. We are in the age of 'big data', which might lead you to believe that qualitative data is redundant. Vast global companies have computer systems that gather, store, slice, dice and aggregate every scrap of data relating to all aspects of their business, from long-term strategy and global market growth predictions to the number of paper clips used only once before being bent out of shape by a not fully engaged participant in a business meeting. Whether you're a customer, supplier, partner or employee, you seemingly can't breathe without someone recording the event on a massive database.

Supermarkets, for example, use loyalty cards to record data that enables them to analyse when, where and how often you shop, in addition to what you buy, what you won't buy, what you'll buy as an alternative if your preferred item isn't available, how much you spend, what will induce you to try something different or more expensive, and what won't — basically, every conceivable purchasing choice you make, might make, or will never make. They gather an unbelievable amount of quantitative data on each and every one of their customers who has a loyalty card, which they then use to run and grow their business.

The reputation of qualitative data as the poor relation is down to the fact that it is, well ... er ... harder to quantify. Qualitative data still has a role to play with Blue Chips though. If you doubt this, consider the supermarket example again. Loyalty cards can give supermarkets all sorts of useful information about your purchasing decisions, but what if you stop using your local supermarket because an employee was rude to you? They can't know this from the data gathered by the loyalty card, and they won't know it from customer complaint data, either, if no one lodged a complaint. All they'll know is that you've stopped shopping with them.

To find out why customers leave, supermarkets would need the story behind the data.

Perhaps they'd ask the opinions of staff and customers locally to help identify and analyse the problem. Then they'd undoubtedly revisit the data to look at it alongside this research. Of course, there is a good chance that any qualitative data they gather they will try to convert to quantitative data somewhere along the line. They do this by aggregating views from many employees or customers. But this data will still have started out as qualitative, and in the conversion to quantitative may even lose some of its meaning.

As a leadership coach, it makes sense to align your coaching with business objectives and measure results using existing business performance indicators. The measurement will be as exact as coaching participants and their line managers can make it through discussion. In trying to get it exact, they'll talk about the challenges participants faced, how the challenges were tackled, and the results they can see and describe. They'll discuss the impact on relevant performance indicators.

Worried that her spectacular results would make her unpopular, Meryl hid her success in an elaborate series of spreadsheets and densely written reports.

This is what business leaders do, day in and day out. They discuss and analyse results to inform planning and decision-making. They're good at it, so get them working for themselves and for you by measuring the results of your leadership coaching. Whether they generate quantitative or qualitative data, or both, they will increase their understanding of what difference your leadership coaching makes to their business.

Our clients at Accelerated Success value the opportunity to measure the results they get through our coaching programmes. It deepens their understanding of the value of leadership coaching and where else in their business they might use it. For us, measuring results provides valuable marketing currency in the form of both data and stories that we use to win further business with the client company and with new clients.

We've walked you through the three phases of our Accelerated Success Process: *Alignment*, *Acceleration* and *Continued Success*. We've emphasised throughout where and how marketing and delivery overlap and enhance each other. Now we need to shift the focus to how you leverage client relationships to help you grow your business.

PART 3
The alligator's dance

*Finally, after much thought and many insights,
the alligator said, 'Now that I know what's what,
I should make use of it all'.*

Marketing your services can be exhausting and demoralising. It may even take over from delivery as your number one priority. You end up putting more thought, time and energy into marketing than you do into the actual business of leadership coaching.

Still, it has to be done. You can't deliver leadership coaching without winning the business first, and when you win new business you immediately have to knuckle down to winning the next bit of business. There's no let-up.

Sometimes it may seem that in setting up your business you have devised an elaborate, marketing-based approach for self-inflicted punishment — stomping all over yourself! There's a simple test you can perform to decide whether that describes you:

If, when you win new business, you feel pleased, thrilled or even jubilant about the win, enthusiastic about delivery, vindicated in your approach to marketing and confident about winning further clients, you're experiencing the joy of running your own business. You're dancing!

If, on the other hand, when you win new business you flip between shrieking ecstasy and tearful relief, and decide to take a few days off from thinking about anything — including delivery or winning further business, just until you can get over the shock — you're probably tending more toward giving yourself a good stomping.

Where are you on the dancing / stomping continuum?

In this section, you will learn how to dance more and stomp less.

HOW DO YOU FEEL ABOUT MARKETING?
SPLAT!!!
Well done!
Dancing
YOUR OWN FOOT
YOU
Stomping
KRO

Chapter 10: Leverage the relationship

Play to your strengths

To be proficient at doing business with Blue Chips and to move away from grinding yourself into the dirt, day after day, you need to do more of the marketing activity that works well and is fun, and less of the stuff that doesn't work so well and leaves you covered in bruises. It's a very simple distinction — leveraging existing client relationships works well, while perpetually targeting and developing new prospects from scratch is harder work and far less successful.

It's the business-to-business relationship that's important here, not the coaching relationship. The business-to-business (B2B) relationship may involve the same people as the coaching relationship (participant and line manager), but the purpose of each is quite different. The coaching relationship is about empowering individual leaders to maximise their contribution to their organisation — usually, the way we do it here at Accelerated Success — over a period of 7-10 months. The B2B relationship is about maximising the value of your service to your client company, ideally over a period of five years or more, and in so doing, maximising your business revenue from this client over the same period.

Professional services such as leadership coaching thrive on building long-term and mutually productive client relationships. These are relationships where you take time to discover your potential clients' challenges, and continue to do this when they are clients. Where your coaching delivers great results that are measurable, and you ensure your client understands the value you bring. Where you help clients identify where else your services can add value. They look to you as a partner and are happy to refer you to leaders in their own and other companies. You keep in touch with decision-makers in your client company, knowing that they likewise benefit from this contact and that they don't see you as a nuisance. Relationships where you generate lots of coaching work and earn good money.

When you have client relationships like this, you really are dancing!

If you don't work in this proactive way, your client relationships can quickly fizzle out or limp along with disappointing levels of further business. You will have sold your clients short and squandered a fantastic marketing opportunity, condemning yourself to the treadmill of perpetually targeting and developing new leads. Stomp! Stomp! Stomp!

At Accelerated Success, developing the right kind of relationship with our clients required a real mind shift. We had to learn to see ourselves as consultants to the company and truly believe that we offered a high-value service that helped them achieve their business objectives.

We had to see ourselves as business partners.

For a long time this felt at odds with the role of being a coach. A real turning point for us came when we researched how our service had added value to our clients. After we analysed and digested their feedback, we realised that it was our responsibility to enable as many leaders as possible to have access to our services. We couldn't do this if we didn't step up with the B2B relationship.

As a leadership coach you are particularly well placed to leverage the B2B relationship. You work with:

Leaders

Leaders in Blue Chips are key decision makers, budget holders and influencers. If they value your leadership coaching and can see where else in their organisation it will add value, they are well placed to commission more — or at least to persuade others in their organisation to do so. As a leadership coach, therefore, you should create opportunities to ensure your clients fully understand the value you bring and help them identify where else in their business they might use your service. If you win new business, both you and your client benefit. If there is no new business to be had at this particular time, at least they've had a reminder that you are there, and they are clear about the value you bring.

Confidentially speaking

If you want to be effective with your marketing, you will need to work to a different set of rules of engagement for the B2B relationship than to those of a coaching relationship. If you don't, you will tend to default to rules that work very well for coaching but are wholly inappropriate for marketing, and that can seriously undermine your business success.

For example, many coaches are understandably concerned about sharing information relating to coaching, for fear of breaking confidentiality. The need for confidentiality between coach and participant in a coaching relationship is absolute — coaching participants MUST be confident that whatever they say in their session will not be shared. The content of coaching discussions is confidential to coach and participant. Sharing this content is unquestionably unethical and unprofessional. If as a coach you ignore this, you will destroy your reputation and your business.

However, there is a clear distinction between the *content* of coaching discussions and the *outcomes* of that coaching. Properly aligning and measuring leadership coaching against business objectives focuses attention on the outcomes of coaching and on business results — the changes the coaching has enabled and improvements in individual, team and business performance. *Content* must not be shared, whereas *outcomes and business results* are visible within an organisation. *Those* can be shared. They relate to performance and can be discussed openly within the normal business context. They can also be written into reports that become useful management information, which can be thrown into the mix for management discussion and analysis to inform planning and decision-making.

Clearly, the sharing of coaching outcomes and business results in written reports still has to be done responsibly. We always show written reports to the individual leaders who achieved the outcomes and results the reports contain. We then ask for permission to share the information with named individuals, such as line managers, colleagues and in human resources. We also tell them the reason we want to share the information, which is to help others in their company understand how they might use our coaching services. This approach gives the leaders involved a chance to change or remove anything they are not comfortable sharing. They very rarely change anything though. They are usually more than happy to let others know about the challenges they faced and the results they have achieved.

Blue Chips thrive on effective sharing of information and go to great lengths and expense to make it happen. There is nothing unethical about sharing information on *coaching outcomes and business results* if done in line with business norms. It is of value to the client company, enabling them to fully understand what they get from leadership coaching and where else they might use it, and is therefore also of value to your coaching business for marketing purposes.

If you want to leverage the B2B relationship with a client company, and sell additional coaching programmes and gain referrals within and outside the company, you need to promote the value of your service to your client. Tell them exactly what they got for their money. If you don't, it won't happen by itself, and it will probably mean that you miss out on further business that is there for the taking.

Use what you have

Word-of-mouth marketing is a powerful thing! It now means any person-to-person promotion, whether spoken or written, and via face-to-face or telephone, text, email or social media. New technology enables viral marketing where companies plant messages that rapidly spread throughout communities or populations person-to-person. A single YouTube clip, for example, might get millions of hits worldwide if it is sufficiently funny, poignant, interesting, or features cats and dogs getting along.

You'd think, therefore, that great results from your leadership coaching would instantly be shared across the closed community of a client company. On the back of one leadership coaching programme, all leaders in the company would know of its success and understand the value of coaching. No need for marketing, because leader-to-leader communication and recommendation will do it for you. Success promotes itself, and leaders across the company are prompted to contact you to enquire about your services.

It sounds somewhat plausible and largely ridiculous. Of *course* it doesn't happen that way! Even when success stories spread, they don't tend to 'go viral', and they certainly don't lead to business prospects hammering at your door. It's not that nobody's interested, just that their focus is on other things — such as the million and one items on their to-do list.

If you don't promote the success of your service and actively seek out further business, nobody else will do it for you. You can use word-of-mouth by way of testimonials to the value of your service, but not before you get the ball rolling.

3-Way meetings

You can make a good start in promoting your success with coaching participants and their line managers via 3-Way meetings and by measuring results. It isn't safe to assume that even participants fully understand what they've learned, what they've changed, and the difference this has made to them and their business — not until you've facilitated a formal review and close that involves their line manager. Neither is it safe to assume that line managers are fully aware of participant achievements. Looking at the progress made, where to go next, and how it all fits in with the bigger picture, is all part of maximising the value of a leadership coaching programme, and of helping everyone else see and understand that value too. It's a great service to clients, and very effective marketing for you.

Report-Back meetings

Once you have measured the results of a coaching programme, without fail you must set up a separate meeting to formally report the success to the buyer — the budget holder who paid for the programme. In cases where the buyer is not the participant's line manager, the Report-Back is particularly important as they will not otherwise know what they got for their money, their return on investment (ROI). Even where the buyer *is* the line manager, you should still have a separate Report-Back meeting. The 3-Way Final Review is focused on the participant's achievements and needs, whereas the Report-Back is an opportunity for the line manager or buyer to focus on the difference the Accelerated Success programme has made to the business, and where further programmes will add value.

This is what makes the Report-Back such a powerful marketing opportunity for you — it is bringing further value to your client, and at the same time maximising your chances of winning more business. Don't overdo it on the Report-Back though. Buyers are busy people, and a Report-Back following each individual coaching programme may not be appropriate. If you are delivering just one programme, always report back. If you are delivering several, report back on all of them together. Your client and you get the same value, but it's a better use of everyone's time.

Also, don't forget that if you conduct Business Value meetings to measure results of a coaching programme 4-6 months after it ends, you can schedule another buyer Report-Back too. The buyer will want to know the long-term impact of any coaching programmes they have paid for.

Report-Back meetings are another opportunity for you to market your services by playing to your strengths as a coach. Once you have taken buyers through a report on participant achievements in one or more coaching programmes, ask them if there is anyone else on their team who would benefit from your service, or any other parts of the business where they need to achieve better results. Use your coaching skills to help them think this through, and offer free Strategy Sessions for them and others in their business if they need further help with the decision. Don't worry that Strategy Sessions are time consuming for you; they're a great tool for winning further business, so this is a valuable use of your time.

At Accelerated Success we work with a small number of client companies at any one time to build long-term and productive relationships. It takes time and effort at first, but it's worth it. Winning further business is now simpler, faster and more fun than when we went the high-volume route — networking and the like. And in some cases clients come to us to request our services, rather than us having to go to them. All this is the result of getting things right from the start and throughout the relationship. Cultivating further business in this way soon becomes a habit you accept as an ongoing business activity, rather than a dreaded occasional event.

Go out there

The same principles apply to asking for referrals. The leader you are referred to will invariably take far more notice of you and your service if you are introduced to them by someone they trust and respect, rather than if you make contact via another route such as cold calling or networking.

If you feel awkward about cultivating further business from a satisfied client, then actively seeking referrals from them can seem like a deadly sin — but it isn't! However, you do have to be careful how you go about it. Some clients will feel comfortable referring you to other leaders they know within and outside their company. Others won't be as comfortable, although they still might happily provide you with testimonials.

Referrals are an excellent way of growing your business, but you have to know exactly who you are looking for and who is a good fit for your service so that you can educate your clients on what a good referral is for you. Simply asking existing clients if they know any leaders they could introduce you to is clumsy and won't work. It is far too unfocused, and immediately puts the people you are asking under pressure. All of a sudden they have to bring to mind any and every leader they have ever known, while simultaneously deciding which, if any, would be a suitable prospect for you, and whether or not those leaders would be happy about being approached in the first place.

Identify your target company

You can greatly improve your chances of success when asking for referrals by having a process and doing your research first. It's worth the effort. You're looking for quality, not quantity — a small number of good referrals with a high probability of converting to paying clients, rather than a large number that don't end up going anywhere.

You can schedule the research in your diary as another ongoing activity, such as coaching sessions, administrative work, marketing and accounts. You want this to become the norm, not an occasional activity that you tend to put off and never actually get around to.

The research can be interesting, combining Internet work and informal discussions with existing clients to:

o   Identify your target company — a company you want to work with

o   Identify your target leader — a leader in the target company who you think will benefit from your leadership coaching service

o   Identify your referrer — a leader you have worked with in an existing client company who knows your prospect

It is essential that you have a clear idea of the sort of company you want to work with (refer back to the *Focus on value* chapter on how to develop your target company profile). Take a look at your existing clients' websites — Blue Chips usually put a great deal of information about their clients, suppliers and partner organisations there. It's useful, and it's free. Research this information and decide which companies fit your target company profile, and are therefore the companies you want as clients. Visit the websites of these other companies to find out more about their vision and mission, the key challenges they face, and how they are tackling them.

It's worth noting that leaders in your client company may be open to providing referrals to a partner or supplier company, but not to their client companies. You don't have to make assumptions about this, but stay sensitive to possible concerns they have when you come to them to ask for referrals. If you sense a reluctance to refer to clients, you can still target the company via an alternative route. To avoid tying yourself up in knots on this one, you could go easy on yourself and have a rule that you don't ask clients for referrals to their clients. It's your choice.

Identify your target leader

Internet research can only take you so far. You will be able to research possible target companies further when you move on to identifying your target leader. As with your target company, it is essential to have a clear idea of the sort of leader you want to work with. (Refer back to the *Focus on value* chapter on developing your target leader profile.)

The best way to unearth the name(s) of possible target leaders in your target companies is to speak to leaders you know in your existing client companies. You already know there is a connection there, because you identified your possible target companies from your clients' websites. Set up a series of informal face-to-face or telephone chats with leaders in your client companies by asking them for 30 minutes for a quick catch-up and to ask their advice on winning business with a new company.

The purpose of these chats is not to ask for a referral, but to gather information about possible target companies and leaders who you might want to do business with. The chats should be with leaders you know and who you think have some sort of connection with your target company. Perhaps they've spoken about the company before, or about a contact they have there, or they used to work there. If you don't know of anyone with a connection, talk to leaders you have worked with who are most likely to know someone in one of these companies. If all else fails, talk to leaders you have worked with who you find easy to talk to. Any one of them should have fairly good knowledge of their company's client, supplier and partner companies.

Before each chat, decide which company you're going to discuss with that particular leader. It's tempting to go in with a long list of companies in an attempt to keep your options open, but this makes it difficult to focus the discussion. You can end up not getting as much from it as you might. Remember, you are not looking for all the answers from one brief chat, just some useful pointers, such as:

> *I'm pretty familiar with that company. They've recently undergone big changes and have a relatively new U.K. management team.*
>
> *Jo in professional services has done a lot of work with them.*
>
> *They're in a complete mess! Don't touch 'em.*

Each of these snippets of information can be very useful to you. Knowing a company has a new management team can help you decide your marketing angle. If you've previously worked with Jo, she may be the right person for you to ask to make a referral. Knowing a company is in complete chaos could save you from wasting a lot of time for no good result.

Of course, you might also get:

Know them? Of course I know them. The new CEO used to be my boss at XYZ. I'd be delighted to introduce you.

Wouldn't that be nice? It does happen occasionally, but it's not something you should bank on. The point is, you don't know what you'll discover, so don't make assumptions.

Informal chats with existing clients are a great way to gather information about potential clients, and to sort the genuinely promising leads from the rest.

Identify your referrer

In addition to helping you identify your target leader(s), your informal chats with existing clients will also help you identify your referrer if there is one. If there isn't a leader in one of your existing client companies who can or is willing to refer you to your target leader in your target company, you can't progress with a referral. Your work isn't wasted, as you now have a lot of useful information you can turn to when the right referrer comes along. Or you can approach your target leader and company via another route, such as direct call or in writing.

Where you do identify a potential referrer, no need to leap straight into asking for a referral. Take time to think about how you will make this request. If you get things right from here, you've got a good chance of winning new business in a new client company. Gold dust! If you make a mess of it, you've just wasted all your hard work and squandered a great business opportunity. It's not easy picking yourself up after that.

Where possible, ask for a referral in person. The conversation is similar whether you are asking for an internal referral to another part of a client business, or an external referral to another company. Where you are aware that your client knows your **target leader** for a referral, you can say:

> *You remember we were talking about company X and you mentioned that you know their CFO? I see they've recently restructured and I know they're trying to push through a lot of changes. Do you think the CFO would be interested in talking with me about the work I've done here with leaders who are driving change? How would you feel about introducing us?*

Where you are aware that your client knows your **target company** for a referral, you can say:

> *I see that company Y has just made an acquisition. You might know that I've done a lot of work with Sally in business operations [Sally is a colleague in their company], transitioning her team leaders into the new set up there. Do you know anyone I might speak to in company Y to see if there is anything I can do to support them?*

If yes:

> *How would you feel about introducing us?*

If no:

> *Have you got any colleagues with good contacts there? How would you feel about putting us in touch?*

The next step is to manage the process proactively to make sure the referral happens. You can suggest to the person who has agreed to make the referral:

> *We have a standard process for referrals. Would it work for you if I draft an email you can edit and send to your contact, which introduces us and what we do?*

> *I will attach an article and a link to relevant success stories on our website. If you can send this to your contact, I will follow up with them only if they come back to you first saying they are happy for me to do so.*

> *When is a good time to do this?*

You will notice we say we will only follow up on a referral once our contact, the person making the referral, has received permission for us to do so from the person they are referring us to. This may seem unnecessarily complicated and doomed to failure. However, we have found referrers and the leaders they refer us to feel more comfortable with this approach. We are successful in winning business in this way, and we don't find ourselves in conversations with leaders who are unhappy because they feel they've been manipulated into talking to us.

Here's an example of a referral email one of our clients wrote for us:

Dear Kamal,

I'd like to make an introduction to you, that I hope might be of interest and relevance to [potential client's company name]. *Sue Burnell is from Accelerated Success (www.acceleratedsuccess.co.uk) and has worked with* [referrer's company name] *for a number of years, at a variety of levels but specifically with key members of the UK Management Team.*

Sue recently helped me with restructuring my team and transitioning in several new account directors, as part of a company acquisition. I thought we would probably miss quarterly targets during this period but business results actually improved, and are continuing to improve in the longer term.

I mentioned to Sue that I felt there was a good degree of synergy between [referrer's company name] *and some of our partners, and suggested that I could potentially introduce Accelerated Success to* [potential client's company name], *and I felt that you were the best initial point of contact. I'd like to suggest that I get Sue to contact you to discuss if her approach could work for you. Can you let me know if you're OK for me to pass on your details?*

Thanks,

Jessica Roberts

Making the connection

If all goes well and your referral target agrees to speak to you, follow up with your own email:

> *Dear Kamal,*
>
> *I'm following up on Jessica Roberts' email introduction of* [date of email]. *We have been working with Jessica's company to help transition in new staff from a recent acquisition to become productive as quickly as possible. Would it be of value to you to set up a 15-minute call to discuss whether we could help you in a similar way?*
>
> *I'm available on Wednesday 24 or Friday 26 September, between 2.00-4.00pm. Would either of these be a good time for me to call you? Please do suggest alternative dates.*
>
> *Regards*

Sometimes potential clients will respond with a firm date and time. Other times they will not reply. Follow up in either case. Have a prepared message you can leave if you don't get to speak to someone in person, saying why you are calling and when you will call again.

When they do take your call, you can help establish rapport quickly by reminding them of your mutual connection and how you helped them. Ask if they have had time to read the article and success stories on your website. The answer will usually be no, but don't let this faze you!

Tell them why you wanted to speak with them and don't assume they have a problem. Say something like:

> *Many organisations experience X, Y and Z when they are in your situation. How have you managed to address that in your company?*

They're likely to be fairly non-committal, although they may open up a little. If you find they are blocking your questions, ask if this isn't a good time. If they're interested in speaking with you, they'll probably warm up or reschedule the call. If they do engage in conversation more freely, take your time — don't forget, you're not asking them to marry you! Not yet, anyway. You just want to find out if there is enough common ground to warrant both of you investing time in a longer meeting.

Have further questions prepared to keep the discussion moving. Also, keep a success story handy, one where you helped another company in a similar situation. If you genuinely think your services can help them, suggest a face-to-face meeting:

> *From what you've said it sounds like there would be value for both of us in having a more detailed conversation. Would you like to set up a meeting?*
>
> *Is this a good time to get a date in the diary?*

When you get your face-to-face meeting, your aim is to get them to agree to a Strategy Session. Ask about their current situation in relation to the challenges you think you can help them overcome. Use any relevant success stories to illustrate your experience and credibility. If you think your services will help them and you want to work with them, offer a Strategy Session:

> *From our discussions so far I think we can help you. What we usually do at this stage is offer a free Strategy Session. The purpose of the session is to give you time to think about your vision and objectives for the next 12-18 months, and to identify your key challenges in achieving them. It will also give you an experience of working with us and the value we add. How does that sound to you?*

When you make it to this stage, wonderful! You know about Strategy Sessions and what they can do for your potential clients and for you. Always, schedule the Strategy Session before you leave the meeting.

The last word on referrals

In practice, asking for referrals is not always as clear cut as we have described here. Referrals are a great way of winning business but there isn't a nice linear approach that always gets results. You will inevitably change tack as you go. Promising leads prove not to be what you thought and fizzle out. On the other hand, completely unexpected opportunities will crop up. Some situations will require you to be very direct, for others you will need to be less so. Sometimes you'll be able to quickly set up calls and meetings, sometimes you won't. Sometimes you'll even get a flat *'no'*.

However, by pursuing referrals, whatever results you get you'll get them quicker and with less effort than if you try to connect with potential clients through standard networking. And where you are successful, you'll be connecting with a leader you know you want to work with, and supported by a personal recommendation from someone that leader respects and trusts.

To succeed with referrals you need to get yourself out there and be resourceful, resilient and flexible. Above all, remember 'the key to the universe' is to always follow up. Try out different approaches and see what works best for you, and for your clients and potential clients. Be sensitive to their possible concerns about making and receiving referrals. Manage those concerns. They are not deal-breakers that mean you shouldn't pursue referrals.

A word of encouragement: This may feel like an alien process, but as a coach you are so well placed to do this work. You know how to listen, as opposed to so many salespeople who don't. Because you listen well, you also know what questions to ask that will get leaders thinking.

Cultivating further business and actively seeking referrals from your existing clients is about asking questions and listening. It's not about selling. Your B2B relationships with clients are a hugely important asset to your business, but you have to make the most of them to benefit your clients, your potential clients and you.

Chapter 11: Plan your transition

If you are like us your coach training and ongoing professional development is important to you — action learning sets, conferences, coaching supervision, qualifications, accreditations, training courses, memberships, discussion forums, reading books and coaching magazines. If you undertake just a few of these activities each year you're investing a lot of time, money and hard work in enhancing your capability as a leadership coach. And you do it because you want to provide the best service possible to your clients.

But what sort of investment do you make each year in developing your marketing capability? Our guess is, considerably less than your professional development, and perhaps not very much at all. These are our top ten suggestions for transferring what you've learned in this book into marketing practice as efficiently and effectively as possible:

1. Don't try and do this work on your own. It is tough, it needs regular attention and you will experience lows as well as highs. Work with at least one other colleague, who is as dedicated as you are to improving their marketing and growing their business.

2. Make working together a priority activity and set aside a regular time each week. Weekly is ideal for taking small steps, often, which really helps you both build momentum. Monthly meetings may feel comfortable but you risk progress being too slow and there is plenty of time to procrastinate and get overwhelmed between meetings.

3. Use Strategy Sessions to help each other in exploring where you are currently and where you want to be with your businesses. You can adapt the questions you use to focus specifically on identifying marketing development needs. Use your coaching expertise to help each other drill down into what are your key challenges in winning business with Blue Chips, and to illuminate the value of improving your marketing capability.

4. Then use the outcome setting process to help each other identify the one area each of you wants to address first. Identify robust measures for progress and achievement against your outcomes, and set realistic timescales to work to. Make a commitment to improving your marketing capability and hold each other accountable for progress and outcomes. When each of you achieves an outcome, move onto the next on your list.

Trying out new approaches in practice is critical and our advice is not to go for too much all at once. Select a low risk situation and decide what you want to try out. Take time to plan and prepare, execute and reflect on the impact of your actions with your coaching partner. Decide how to improve your approach and repeat the cycle. This way you will experience improvement over time, continuously building on your competence and confidence. Remember, getting better at marketing is like becoming a better coach, something you will always be working on.

5. A colleague who has worked with us to adapt our approach to her own coaching practice shares this advice.

> *When you try out new approaches on existing clients, this is not only part of your transition, it is a transition for your client too. Attend to this when you are planning to experiment with new approaches — look after your clients and make sure they're getting value.*
>
> *You don't have to begin at the beginning. For example, if a client is part way through a programme, experiment with the progress review. See how it works for your client and for you. If you're coming to the end of a coaching programme or have recently finished one, think about how you can use measuring success or business value meetings. Obviously, if you're just starting out with a programme, you can use outcome setting to align the coaching with the participant's business objectives.*

> *I have found it very easy to adapt individual steps in the Accelerated Success Process to fit with how I'm already working with existing clients. You can do this for any stage in the process.*

6. If you get stuck, and you will, supervision is an appropriate space to work on issues which may present as marketing but are more to do with mindset and limiting assumptions. Supervision can often illuminate areas which need attending to and go beyond knowing your value and having good processes. A fear of rejection and a fear of success are just a couple of common issues coaches may need to attend to in relation to marketing efforts.

7. It can be very helpful to get yourself a mentor. By that we mean someone who has expertise in selling and marketing, who is prepared to spend time with you thinking through and commenting on live marketing initiatives. We have had the benefit of a skilled and generous mentor who has educated and guided us over the last 10 years. We don't have a formal arrangement but we do have access to him when we need insight which is beyond our expertise.

8. In addition to informal support, be prepared to pay for your marketing education. Invest time and money in yourself and your willingness to learn because you will get there faster working with the right support. You could participate in a formal marketing programme that combines training, education, coaching on live marketing

issues and mentoring. This could be virtual or face-to-face. You will find programmes that are specifically aimed at coaches and others that are more generally for small professional service businesses.

Be critical when deciding how to spend your money though. Many sites make promises about achieving a six figure income with speed and ease. In reality, if you want to grow your business it will take a lot of hard work. Go for the learning opportunities that help you direct your effort effectively, not the ones that promise great results without having to put in the hard yards.

9. Read books on marketing and selling — we've added some books we found particularly useful in *Chapter 13, Additional Resources*, at the end of this book. Find an eZine or blog you like and sign up for free articles and tips. Twitter can also be a great place for regular, bite sized tricks and tips, and links to further information. Join a marketing action learning set or set one up. Attend webinars. Think about marketing, talk about marketing and, whatever you do, don't forget to try things out. There is no one right place to start improving your marketing capability. Trust your own judgement and begin where ever feels right to you.

10. Aim for a series of small improvements over the long term, not marketing nirvana in six months. Don't wait until you have perfected your approach in one area before moving onto the next. Make enough progress and move on. All of the areas are connected and you will

find that improvement in one area influences your performance in another. Be realistic with your expectations and the timescales you are working to and most important be kind and understanding of yourself — marketing is tough and can be scary. However, people just like you learn to get really good at it and realise they enjoy it.

12: Quick Guides

Quick Guides contain:

○ Preparatory questions contained in the worksheets that we send to participants prior to set-agenda meetings.

○ Some suggested supplementary questions (*in italics*) for the coach to use in meetings to dig deeper around each worksheet question.

There are Quick Guides for:

1. Strategy Session
2. 3-Way Start Up
3. Outcome Setting
4. 3-Way Progress Review
5. Measuring Success
6. Sustaining Growth
7. 3-Way Final Review
8. Business Value

Pdf versions of Quick Guides, plus other advice and resources for marketing and delivering leadership coaching to Blue Chips, are available from our website at **www.bluechipcoaching.co.uk**.

Quick Guide 1

Strategy Session

1. What's the purpose of your part of the business?

    Tell me more.

2. Describe how you fit into the organisation, including who you report to, the size of your team, and budget / revenue generation responsibilities.

    Tell me more.

3. What's your vision for your part of the business?

    Tell me more.

    What's important to you in your work?

4. What are your key objectives for the next 12-18 months?

    Tell me more about each objective in turn.

5. What are the 3 or 4 most important and challenging areas of your role in fully achieving these objectives?

    Tell me more about each area in turn.

6. What would it be most important for you to get better at, to significantly improve performance in these areas? Try to select something that will extend your capability as a leader / key player, rather than something technical you can accomplish by learning a new skill.

    Coach asks about what participant needs to get better at in each challenging area in turn, starting with the most important:

What's the one area, that if you made significant gains here, it would be a big deal for you personally and add value to the business?

Tell me more about this.

Coach digs into participant's PAIN:

How do you know this is a problem?

What are the visible effects of this problem in the business?

If you don't get better in this area, what happens?

And then what happens? And what does that affect?

Coach helps participant visualize the GAIN:

What would getting better in this area allow YOU to do, which you can't do today?

Where do the benefits of being able to do this show up?

What will it allow the business to do, which it can't do today?

Where do the benefits of the business being able to do this show up?

Coach focuses participant on the VALUE of making change:

What's the value of addressing this area?

What is the ultimate gain for you? Your team? Your line manager? The wider business? Your customers?

Coach reconnects participant with the situation now:

What has stopped you and / or the business from addressing this area before?

Where are you on a scale of 1-10, where 10 means it is critical that you address this area and 1 is the opposite?

Quick Guide 2

3-Way Start Up

At your Strategy Session we considered the one area, that if you made significant gains here, it would be a big deal for you personally and add value to the business. We explored how things are now and how you would like them to be.

1. Assuming you make progress in this area, what can you reasonably expect to see changing over the next 3-4 months?

    To participant:

    > *Tell us more about this.*
    >
    > *How will things be different for you? Your team? Your line manager? The wider business? Your customers?*

    To line manager:

    > *What's your view on this?*

2. How will you know if you are making progress or not?

    To participant:

    > *Tell us more about this.*

    To line manager:

    > *What's your view on this?*

3. What ways could you measure progress in this area? Brainstorm and make a list. Think about quantitative indicators such as targets, margin, time spent on important tasks and customer feedback. Also think

about qualitative indicators such as levels of stress, job satisfaction, collaboration and morale.

To participant:

Where are you against these indicators now?

Ideally, where do you want to be against these indicators in 12 months' time?

To line manager:

What's your view on this?

Are these indicators of progress appropriate? Are they within [participant's name] *sphere of influence? Are* [participant's name] *12 month targets realistic? How do you think* [participant's name] *business objectives will be impacted?*

4. How will making progress help you achieve your business objectives?

To participant:

Tell us more about this.

To line manager:

What's your view on this?

5. How will working on this area extend your capability as a leader?

To participant:

Tell us more about this.

To line manager:

What's your view on this?

Quick Guide 3

Outcome Setting

Participants have completed a Strategy Session questionnaire, a Strategy Session and Report-Back, and a 3-Way Start Up worksheet and meeting. The job of the coach is to help participants come up with a clear and measurable outcome they're happy with, one that makes sense based on all the thinking, discussion and learning they've done up to this point.

> *We've discussed the one area, that if you made significant gains here, it would be a big deal for you personally and add value to the business.*
>
> *Now we need to identify an outcome for you to work towards in the first 3-4 months of your coaching programme. In three or four sentences, summarise the outcome you want in addressing this area.*
>
> *Make sure your sentences are stated positively — tell me what you want, rather than what you don't want. We'll work on the wording together, so don't worry about getting it right the first time.*

Once participants have articulated the outcome they want, the coach helps them finalise how they will measure their achievement against this outcome.

> *Based on our previous discussions, how will you measure achievement against this outcome?*
>
> *What will be the impact on your business objectives?*

Quick Guide 4

3-Way Progress Review

1. What progress have you made towards achieving your outcome?

   To participant:

   > *Tell us more about this.*

   To line manager:

   > *What's your view on this?*

2. What have you done that is helping you achieve your outcome? Think about specific actions / initiatives you have taken, practices you have put in place, and behaviours or new approaches you have adopted.

   To participant:

   > *Tell us more about this.*

   To line manager:

   > *What's your view on this?*

3. Looking at the indicators you identified for measuring achievement towards your outcome, where are you against these indicators now? Refer to your coaching record to help you here.

   To participant:

   > *Tell us more about this.*

   To line manager:

   > *What's your view on this?*

4. Where do you want to be against these indicators by the end of your programme?

   To participant:

> *Tell us more about this.*

To line manager:

> *What's your view on this?*

5. What can you reasonably expect to see changing over the next 3-4 months?

   To participant:

   > *Tell us more about this.*

   To line manager:

   > *What's your view on this?*

6. How will you know if you are making progress or not?

   To participant:

   > *Tell us more about this.*

   To line manager:

   > *What's your view on this?*

7. How is working towards your outcome helping you achieve your business objectives?

   To participant:

   > *Tell us more about this.*

   To line manager:

   > *What's your view on this?*

8. How is working towards your outcome helping you extend your capability as a leader?

   To participant:

   > *Tell us more about this.*

   To line manager:

   > *What's your view on this?*

Quick Guide 5

Measuring Success

1. To what extent have you fully achieved your outcome(s)? Rate yourself on a scale of 1-10, where 10 is fully achieved and 1 is the opposite.

   Tell me more about this.

2. What have you done that has helped you achieve your outcome(s)? Think about specific actions / initiatives you have taken, practices you have put in place, and behaviours or new approaches you have adopted.

   Tell me more about this.

3. Looking at the indicators you identified for measuring achievement towards your outcome(s), where are you against these indicators now? Refer to your coaching record to help you here.

   Tell me more about this.

4. Where were you against these indicators when you began your coaching programme? Refer to your coaching record to help you here.

   Tell me more about this.

5. What other evidence is there to demonstrate your achievement towards your outcome(s)? Think about what is happening differently. Also think about how your team, your line manager, others in the business and customers would answer this question.

   Tell me more about this.

6. How has working towards your outcome(s) helped you achieve your business objectives?

    Tell me more about this.

7. How has achieving against your outcome(s) helped you extend your capability as a leader? Think of specific examples.

    Tell me more about this.

Quick Guide 6

Sustaining Growth

1. What changes have you made that are still not business-as-usual for you? Think about specific actions / initiatives you have taken, practices you have put in place, and behaviours or new approaches you have adopted.

    Tell me more about this.

2. How will you ensure these changes become business-as-usual for you?

    Tell me more about this.

3. What else do you need to work on over the next 3-4 months to build on your achievements during your coaching programme?

    Tell me more about this.

4. How will you know if you are making progress or not?

    Tell me more about this.

5. What ways could you measure progress? Brainstorm and make a list. Think about quantitative indicators such as targets, margin, time spent on important tasks and customer feedback. Also think about qualitative indicators such as levels of stress, job satisfaction, collaboration and morale.

    Where are you against these indicators now?

    Ideally, where do you want to be against these indicators in 3-4 months' time?

6. How will building on your coaching programme in these ways help you achieve your business objectives?

    Tell me more about this.

7. How will building on your coaching programme in these ways help you extend your capability as a leader?

    Tell me more about this.

Quick Guide 7

3-Way Final Review

The 3-Way Final Review is an often rare opportunity for participants to have a high quality performance and feedback discussion with their line manager. Based on discussions at their Measuring Success and Sustaining Growth meetings, participants discuss with their line manager results they have achieved through their coaching programme, providing evidence to back up their claims.

The meeting promotes effective communication between participant and line manager, and supports future planning and decision making. It also clearly demonstrates what difference the coaching programme has made for participants and the wider business. This is where participants and their line manager get to understand business value of the coaching programme. It is also where the coach gathers data and success stories that can be used for marketing purposes.

1. Summarise the outcome(s) you have been working on and to what extent you have fully achieved them.

   To participant:

   Tell us more about each outcome in turn.

   To line manager:

   What's your view on this?

2. What have you done that has helped you achieve your outcome(s)? Think about specific actions / initiatives you

have taken, practices you have put in place, and behaviours or new approaches you have adopted.

To participant:

> *Tell us more about each outcome in turn.*
>
> *What else has helped you achieve your outcome(s)? Think of influences that weren't down to you or to the changes you made.*

To line manager:

> *What's your view on this?*

3. Looking at the indicators you identified for measuring achievement towards your outcome(s), where were you against these indicators at the start of your programme? Where are you now? Give examples of pain-points you have relieved, benefits you have delivered and the business value of these changes.

To participant:

> *Tell us more about each outcome in turn.*

To line manager:

> *What's your view on this?*

4. What else do you need to work on over the next 3-4 months to build on your achievements during your coaching programme? How will you do this? What support do you need and from whom? Refer to your sustaining growth plan.

To participant:

> *Tell us more about this.*

To line manager:

> *What's your view on this?*

5. How has working towards your outcome(s) helped you achieve your business objectives? Think about specific actions / initiatives you have taken, practices you have put in place, and behaviours or new approaches you have adopted.

    To participant:

    > *Tell us more about this.*
    >
    > *What other areas of your work have been impacted?*
    >
    > *Why is this important? Where does the value of that show up?*

    To line manager:

    > *What's your view on this?*

6. How has achieving against your outcome(s) helped you extend your capability as a leader? Think of specific examples.

    To participant:

    > *Tell us more about this.*

    To line manager:

    > *What's your view on this?*

7. What contribution has your Accelerated Success programme made to your progress? Think about what you would have done anyway and what you have achieved above and beyond that.

    To participant:

    > *Tell us more about this.*
    >
    > *What benefits has your programme delivered that you didn't expect?*

What has that given you? What has that enabled you to do? What difference has it made to the wider business? Why is this important?

To line manager:

What's your view on this?

Quick Guide 8

Business Value

1. On a scale of 1-10 where 10 is I have been completely successful and 1 is the opposite, rate where you are against your sustaining growth plan. Think about what you have been working on and what has become business-as-usual.

2. Say some more about why you selected this rating.

   Tell me more about this.

3. Looking at the indicators you identified for measuring progress, where are you against these indicators now? Refer to your sustaining growth plan and worksheet.

   Tell me more about this.

4. Where were you against these indicators when we agreed your sustaining growth plan? Refer to your sustaining growth plan and worksheet.

   Tell me more about this.

5. How have you built on the achievements you made through your coaching programme?

   Tell me more about this.

6. How has this contributed to achieving your business objectives?

   Tell me more about this.

7. How has it helped you extend your capability as a leader?

   Tell me more about this.

8. What was the Accelerated Success programme for you?
    Tell me more about this.

9. What were the three most important things the programme helped you achieve?
    Tell me more about this.

10. What about the programme worked well for you?
    Tell me more about this.

11. What could we improve on?
    Tell me more about this.

13: Additional Resources

Useful links and further reading to help you grow your leadership coaching business working with Blue Chips.

1. Keep a copy of **The Leaderhship Coaching Alligator Handbook** with you at all times. Refer to the different content and Quick Guides when you need them. Use it as your guide to winning business and building long term and productive relationships with Blue Chip clients. Further copies, in eBook and printed format, are available at **www.bluechipcoaching.co.uk**.

2. For examples of **client success stories** for leadership coaching visit our website at **www.acceleratedsuccess.co.uk**. Our site is built around our success stories but it also contains marketing articles and an Accelerated Success programme overview that clients and potential clients can download.

3. For **free resources for coaches** who want to do business with Blue Chips, including pdf versions of the Quick Guides in this book, visit our website at **www.bluechipcoaching.co.uk**. Join our community of leadership coaches and share knowledge and support each other in growing your leadership coaching businesses.

4. For **help with writing an article** to market your leadership coaching visit Jami Bernard's website at **www.barncatpublishing.com**. Writing an article about your services gives you something of value to send potential clients. It also serves as a good starting point for developing your value statement and other marketing material. Jami helped us at Accelerated Success write our marketing articles and this book.

5. For additional **marketing articles and resources for professional service businesses** visit Robert Middleton's website at **www.actionplan.com**. In particular, the back catalogue of blog posts provides a free encyclopaedia on marketing. It's an easy read and packed full of helpful information.

6. To learn more about **getting the attention of leaders** in Blue Chips read *Selling to Big Companies* by Jill Konrath, published by Kaplan. Step-by-step guide with scripts and templates that will help you get your foot in the door with Blue Chips. We refer to it all the time.

7. To learn more about **relationship selling** read *Let's Get Real or Let's Not Play* by Mahan Khalsa and Randy Illig, published by Portfolio. A very practical guide to leveraging buyer / seller relationships that we have read and re-read many times.

8. To learn more **about helping adults identify and address development needs** read *Immunity to Change* by Robert Kegan and Lisa Laskow Lahey, published by Harvard

Business Press. This book has had a strong influence on the questions we use in our Strategy Session.

9. To learn more about **collecting evidence for improved performance** read *All You Need To Know About Action Research* by Jean McNiff and Jack Whitehead, published by Sage. This book has significantly influenced our whole approach to delivering leadership coaching.